BASIC DESIGN

KENNETH F. BATES OWLS IN A TREE ENAMEL PLAQUE

KENNETH F. BATES

Basic Design

PRINCIPLES AND PRACTICE

FOREWORD BY *William M. Milliken*

FUNK & WAGNALLS
NEW YORK

The quotation on pages 114-115 is from Thomas Munro: *The Arts and Their Interrelations.* New York 1949. Reprinted by permission of the publishers, The Liberal Arts Press, Inc.

The picture on page 125 is from *Scientist's Choice,* edited by Franklyn M. Branley, Hayden Planetarium, Basic Books, Inc., publishers.

Published in Canada by

Fitzhenry & Whiteside Limited, Toronto

Library of Congress Catalog Card Number: 74-25356

Republished, 1970

ISBN 0-308-10185-5

CONTENTS

FOREWORD

THE distinction that so many people make between the so-called major and minor arts has always seemed to me to be a fallacious one. Art is art. Size, technique, medium are unimportant. What the artist has wrought by his imagination, what he has fashioned through the technical means at his disposal is the criterion which determines whether art is major or minor.

As the Director of an important museum during long years of an active life, one becomes increasingly conscious of this fact and of the fact that through the ages there have been many emphases in many different parts of the world at many different times. The architecture of Ur of the Chaldees has disappeared but the gold which survived places their artists among the creative geniuses of all time. Could one call that a minor art? Irish illuminators in books such as the Book of Kells raised the Illuminated Manuscript to a level which has never been excelled. Ceramics, ivories, mosaics, painting, sculpture, architecture, each in their time have been major pawns in the agelong pageant of history.

A museum should be a living world. There the art of the past and of the present live together. That has been the ideal that has motivated The Cleveland Museum of Art through the more than forty-five years of its existence.

Life is change—"becoming" in the philosophic sense of that word. Genius is quicksilver. It is never static, for stagnation is death.

It is for that reason that one can never be unduly arbitrary about styles. Technical means can be described. Certain basic principles can be formulated. But genius can break man-made rules to lead into a new-found world. That has been the lesson of history.

Kenneth F. Bates in this excellent book does not say how things should be done. He does not make that mistake. He makes it clear that his book is no do-it-yourself project. He emphasizes general rules which are the backbone of style in all ages. But he never lays down hard and fast precepts which cannot be departed from.

Gertrude Stein in a lecture to The Print Club of Cleveland at The Cleveland Museum of Art made a statement which applies. "I like museums because they have windows which you can look out of." Kenneth Bates has written a book which gives you unending vistas into new worlds too, but he is wise and clever enough to leave it to the individual to apply those principles. He is never dogmatic. It is in this clear call to individual initiative and for the necessity of that individual initiative that his book is immensely helpful.

WILLIAM MATHEWSON MILLIKEN
Director Emeritus
The Cleveland Museum of Art

❧ INTRODUCTION

IT MUST be apparent to the most casual observer of conditions in this country that a peculiar and unprecedented phenomenon has taken place in the past decade. This phenomenon is the do-it-yourself movement. Now "do-it-yourself" may have its rewards. It is obviously the outcome of our continued effort to make better use of the newly added leisure hours of the work week. Whether it is building a bookcase without the help of a carpenter, installing a lawn sprinkler system without employing a plumber, or trying one's hand at making ceramic ash trays, there is no real harm in trying and many feel they have unearthed hidden talents. But the do-it-yourself movement has reached Frankensteinian proportions to the point where almost anything we want to cook, build, or create can be found in a package at the Hobby Convention. Difficulty and disappointment are ahead for the person who does not realize that taste and some sense of design are required to succeed, especially if the "package deal" has anything to do with art. The directions for framing pictures, making mosaics, silk-screen Christmas cards, and dozens of objects involving craft techniques are usually included in the kit, but little aid is given to the purchaser in the way of design. If suggestions for design are given they are often in bad taste and are purposely intended to be copied. Rarely is one expected to create an original design. The would-be artist-craftsman only imagines he is doing creative work and soon discovers that his lack of understanding or formal training in the principles of basic design is a major handicap.

This book has something to do with the "do-it-yourself" situation in America today. There are endless numbers of people who seem to be playing around the fringes of art without the slightest knowledge or background in the subject, and they are dismayed to find that compliments are not always forthcoming even from their most charitable friends. The trifler in art has reached an impasse. Either the hobbyist must chose outlets other than art for his newly acquired leisure hours, or else he must make up his mind to seek some information from art schools and professionals, or at least do some research on his own. The printed label on the carton, the ballyhoo in the store window, and the convincing advertisement insist that no training, no special talent or ability is needed if you merely follow directions. As long as this situation prevails I feel there is need for a book explaining as simply and as concisely as possible some of the basic design principles.

The vastness of the study of design leaves one with a feeling of humility. Design styles and mannerisms change constantly. Each year reveals new ways of reacting to the life about us and each year brings new liberations for the artist—liberations disclosed by such well-known exemplars as Picasso, Braque, Klee, and Leger. Also there are the rediscoveries, the reconsiderations of past civilizations. The undeniable charm of the primitive cave paintings, the present-day interest in African sculpture and other indigenous craft expressions such as the Northwest Indian's totem pole motifs and calligraphic pottery designs are only a few of our revived inheritances which have a particular relationship to our modern sense of taste. And in addition to the designer's rich and varied vocabulary left by past civilizations, our most inexhaustible source of inspiration is nature herself. There are so many kinds of sedges, seed pods, insects, reptiles, birds, flowers, leaves, animals, and human beings which we have failed to observe or utilize as design motifs that the artist's life cannot fail to be one which is crowded with creative thought and enthusiasm for work.

This book is intended for beginning students in design as well as professionals, amateurs, and laymen. I have purposely deleted over-subtle distinctions and hairsplitting discriminations better known to the advanced student of aesthetics. I hope that those who read this book will be inspired to try their own hand at design experiences and not merely look at pictures of other people's work, or read and talk about them. Within all human beings there are unexpressed reactions to the natural forces and effects seen in everyday life. May not some of those people who have never dared to express their design inspirations arrive at something creative and genuine?

It is my conviction that theory without practice has little meaning for the creative artist and that the reverse of this statement is also true. My intention, therefore, is to suggest means of practice and types of problems which utilize these theories. In some cases I have shown how the art student has solved a certain design problem, and how professional artists *might* solve the same problem. I stress the "might" for we have arrived at a period in the history of art which could be called "Specialized Individualism." The artist has always considered himself individualistic, but often willing to follow this or that school of thought. Today each artist attempts to be a specialist establishing his own "school of thought." Consequently, to show or to presume to tell one exactly "how to design" is neither possible nor advisable.

This book is not intended to be a "how-to-do-it" book. It might better be called a "why-to-do-it" book. For this reason the application of design principles to practical problems follows the theoretical approach. My belief is that it is better to probe the making of a design which has no other purpose than creative expression before one attempts to make a "design of a thing." I hope this attitude about design will inspire the reader to search for new directions, new devices, new techniques, and new means of expressing that which he wishes to say.

Today's tendency toward "Specialized Individualism" has brought forth a super-sophistication that sometimes leaves a wide breach between the artist and the unsophisticated layman. Such a breach, I feel, can only be lessened by a greater understanding on the part of the layman of the principles of basic design, and how the contemporary artist makes use of them, or *intentionally* misuses them.

But due to the current emphasis on "the undesigned look" or freedom of expression, it would seem unwise to lay too much stress on what is *"bad"* and what is *"good"* in design. At least, no book should attempt to prove this by inflexible academic standards. At the same time the layman and student need to be informed that there *are* standards in design. These are basic and have never changed throughout history. By comparing two solutions for the same design problem it may be possible to prove by analysis that one is better than the other, although the element of personal taste is not to be denied. The "bad" design may have more appeal than the "right" design.

In the illustrations of recognized masterpieces both historic and contemporary, I have tried to show how the artist makes use of "laws" which govern balance, rhythm, opposition, etc. rather than following "rules" for design. These laws are of cosmic derivation—they are related to the universe. They evolve from our constant association with gravity, the forces of air, light, movement, growth, etc. The artist being both visual and sensitive cannot escape applying these laws to his creative work. For they are the essence of design. Upon what other basis may we judge *both* the Greek horse designed in the fifth century B.C. and the contemporary work of art?

I wish to acknowledge my indebtedness first to my patient and constructive wife, Charlotte, who has been my "home editor," and then to David Keightley, my respected "office editor" at The World Publishing Company. I am grateful for the knowledge and skill in the art of photography shown in the work of Geoffry Landesman who made the majority of photographs in this book, to Soichi Sonami, the photographer for the Museum of Modern Art, and Richard Godfrey of The Cleveland Museum of Art.

I would also like to express my gratitude to the Cleveland Institute of Art, the Metropolitan Museum of Art, The Primitive Museum, The Butler Institute of American Art, The Cleveland Museum of Art, the Museum of Modern Art, the Museum of Contemporary Crafts, the *Craft Horizons* Magazine, the American Craftsmen's Council, and most particularly to the many distinguished contemporary artists and students who are my friends, and who have so generously allowed me to show examples of their work.

BASIC DESIGN

CHAPTER I

DESIGN IN ITS SIMPLEST FORM

Spot, line, shape

How can we start our first lesson in design? How can we come to this subject feeling free and willing to express what we wish to say? Our aim is simplicity, not confusion or frustration. We want to make something which is in good taste, and which will be contemporary in spirit. In order to do this we should start at the very beginning. Let us start with something very simple. Fig. 1.

Simplicity is a word which has been used by artists and aestheticians for many centuries and remains a principle of primary concern. What does the artist or the designer mean when he applies the word "simple" to a work of art? He is not speaking of mental deficiency in the manner of describing a simpleton or a Simple Simon. "Simple" in art means uncomplicated, clarified, or perhaps reduced to the fewest possible lines, shapes, and colors. In order for these elements of a design to communicate to the observer at first glance, they must not be lost in a maze of extraneous and nonessential elaboration. A good design is one to which no more can be added, and at the same time, one from which nothing can be subtracted without causing an emptiness or feeling of incompletion.

Fig. 1. Plain Hacha, Vera Cruz, Mexico, 300–900 A.D. This is still a head, though shape and proportions are strikingly simplified.

In the beginning we are confronted with the piece of paper and the pointed instrument, the pencil; or with the canvas and the brush; and then, there is our mind, our intellect, or our desire to create something. As students of design, however, we would be wise to first explore the making of a "design" before applying this knowledge to the making of a "design of a thing."

SPOT

If we were asked to create the simplest thing possible with pencil and paper, or brush and canvas, it would require merely touching the canvas or paper once. This mark which we would make we will call a "spot" (not a "dot" which usually implies a circular shape).

The spot is of little intrinsic interest, but acquires aesthetic value immediately upon being placed on the page. In the direct center of the page it seems to be quiet and static. Fig. 2. Lower down on the page it seems to be falling (Fig. 3) and above center it appears to rise. Close to the margin it is more conspicuous than when further away from it. Fig. 4. When the spot is large, it comes forward, and when it is tiny it appears to be floating away from us in space. Fig. 5. In the corners it seems to move toward the point and looks as if the edges of the page were pinching it like a nutcracker.

We have spoken only about a large or a small spot which involves size or area. More than one spot of the same size in a variety of groupings could create an interesting pattern (Fig. 6), but by varying the size our grouping is more entertaining. Fig. 7. In addition the spot might take on another characteristic—that of "shape"—a variation of contour. Such variation adds further possibilities. Fig. 8. The variation of size and/or shape might be in a regular progression, large to small, small to large, or at random. Progressions or sequences of spots from large to small, small to large, dark to light, etc., are important to the designer, but only as a principle. Overuse of such a device becomes a

Fig. 2. In the center of the page on the left the spot has little significance, except that of becoming "static." Fig. 3. Here the spot seems to be falling. Fig. 4. The spot which is near the edge attracts more attention than the one further from the edge. Fig. 5. If we think of the white paper as space or atmosphere the tiny spot appears to be floating away from us.

cliché, and in questionable taste. When the device is used with discrimination, however, the eye has a tendency to travel along the progressive steps until it observes the resolution of the sequence. This, one could say, "moves" the eye in one direction or another, and therefore overcomes a static quality in the

Fig. 6. Identical spots at odd intervals on a given page.

Fig. 7. A more fascinating design—the variation of "size."

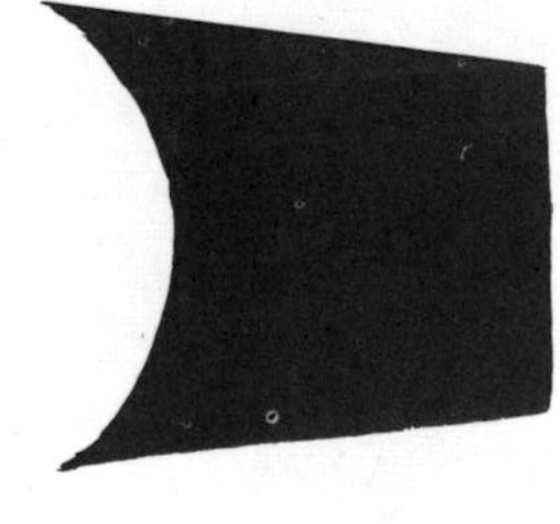

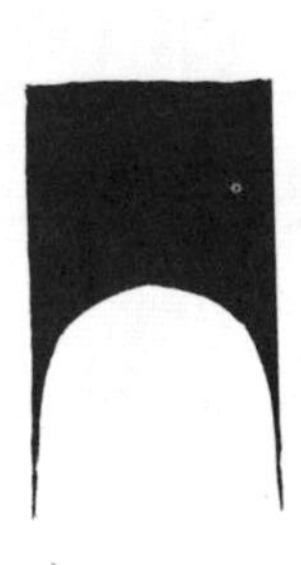

Fig. 8. Our original spots have now been changed in "shape."

composition. Of common occurrence in nature are the progressions of size and shape from the mature seed pod at the bottom of the branch to the unfolded embryonic state at the very tip, such as ripe wheat heads or corn kernels. In certain flowers the sequence progresses in all directions from a central spot rather than in a line. Color progressions (that is, colors going from green to blue to purple, etc.) tend to lead the eye from the beginning of a sequence to its termination.

As we diverge from a round spot to a spot of different shape another possibility arises—that of movement or direction. Fig. 9. We can see that a circular spot does not "move" to the eye. It remains where we place it. A spot with a point, however, goes in the direction of the blunt end if we think of it as a drop of water

Fig. 9. This grouping of spots shows change of "direction."

Fig. 10. These spots show a change in "position."

or a comet; or it can move in the direction of the sharp end if we think of it as a tack or arrowhead.

We have still not exhausted the possibilities for variation and manipulation of the simple spot. The space between one spot and another is important. Spots of the same size, shape, and direction may yet create the most fascinating arrangement if we skillfully plan the distances between individual spots or their position on the page. Figs. 10, 38. The spots may be "far apart" (Fig. 11), which is a term given to things placed at a distance from each other greater than either of their diameters. In such an arrangement there is a feeling of spaciousness. When "near together," the objects are placed at a distance less than their respective diameters or breadth. Fig. 12. Spacing of the spots determines the looseness or the crowded look of our design. There is no set of rules which furnishes the answer regarding space between

Fig. 11. With spots far apart the white paper becomes important.

Fig. 12. Spots near together increase the sense of unity.

Fig. 13. When spots touch there is a feeling of tension.

Fig. 14. Overlapping spots seem to exist in more than one plane.

spots. You, as an artist, must decide this point. Juxtaposition, or "touching," will produce other aspects of the design such as a feeling of tension or collision. Fig. 13. When the spots are "overlapped" one spot may hide the other, or the back one may show through for a transparent effect. Fig. 14.

Explore some of these simple ideas regarding the spot. Fig. 15. Let the ideas about the spot increase your means of expression and relate them to your everyday life. You may discover that suddenly when you look at a slice of Swiss cheese it is no longer just a slice of cheese to you, but a fascinating arrangement of spots. Fig. 16. This is the kind of unplanned, organic design which should have some meaning to you. The same would hold true regarding the subtle difference between leopard's spots and giraffe's spots, the designs in the constellations, variations in knotty pine, or sparrow's eggs. As a designer—as an artist—you should see beyond the accepted appearance of nature.

Fig. 15. Joan Miro, "The Beautiful Bird Revealing the Unknown to a Pair of Lovers"—Imagination and invention with size, shape, position, and direction of the spot motif.

Fig. 16. Swiss cheese takes on aesthetic significance. Some spots touch, some are far apart, some near together, and some overlap.

LINE

The spot alone and its infinite variations would provide inspirational materials for years. We saw that touching the paper or canvas once constituted the spot, theoretically. Now suppose we touch the paper twice. These two spots create a distance between them, or, in other words, the start and finish of a "line." It is axiomatic that to get from one spot to the other by the shortest route results in a mechanically straight line. To the traveler this short route suggests economy of time and speed. To the artist the straight line may not suggest speed as effectively as the line which is slightly curved (streamline). Fig. 17. Our concern as designers is about how this line makes us *feel,* our own individual reaction to its physical structure. Skill needed to produce the line should be forgotten at this point. The often-heard expression "I could never be an artist—I can't draw a straight line" is absurd. The artist never has to draw a straight line—he has a ruler. If one were able to draw a perfectly straight line, but had little concern for what it expressed, he would be less of an artist than one who could not draw a straight line at all.

We are confronted with an inexhaustible number of ways in

Fig. 17. Speed or movement is best shown by slightly curved lines.

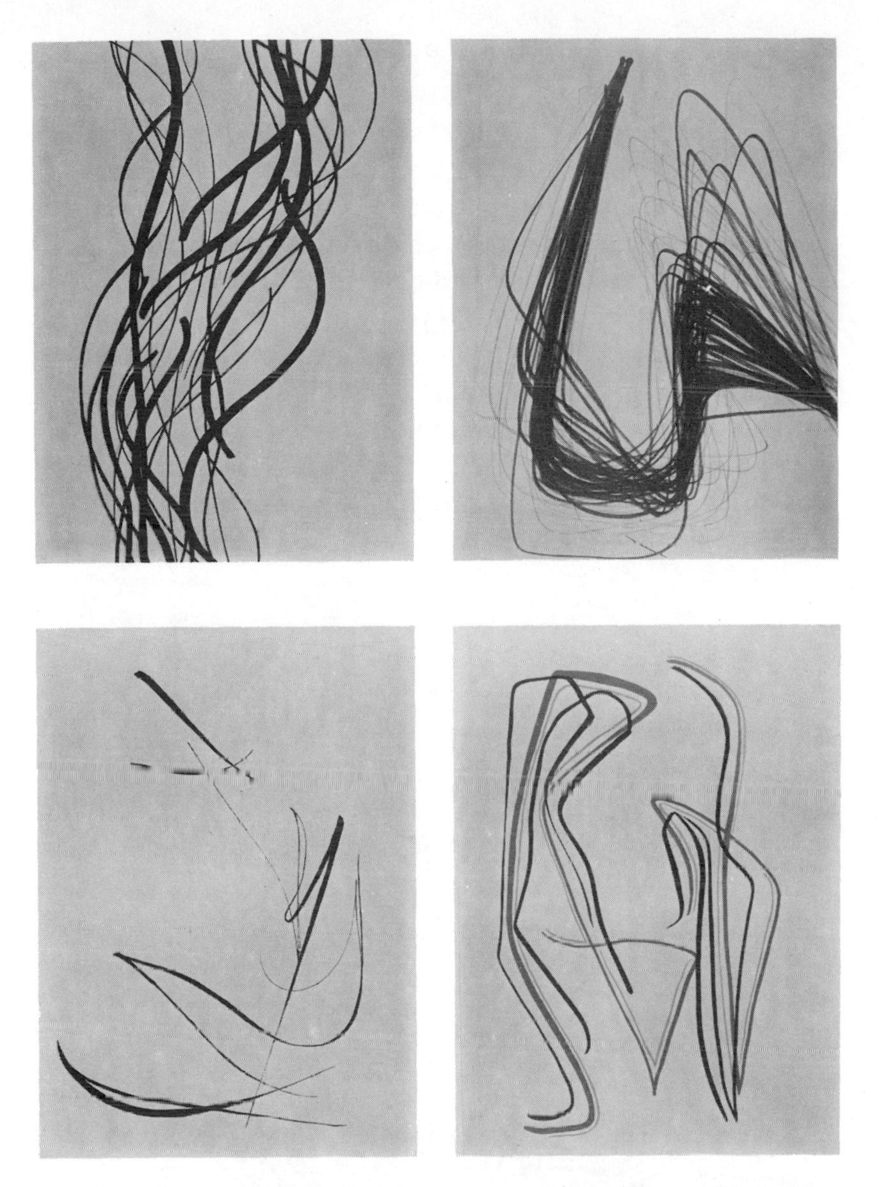

Fig. 18. These could be called fast compound-curved lines. Their slight curvature suggests the paths of smoke. Fig. 19. The greater amount of curvature in these slow compound-curved lines denies the sense of speed. Fig. 20. Rhythm presupposes that we have more than one of a thing, as in this pleasing arrangement of six curved lines. Fig. 21. Bent lines, unlike curved lines, have straight parts and a variety of angles.

which our eye can travel from the beginning of the line to the end of it. Let us try to categorize some of these *lines.* First, there is the straight line, and then the slightly curved or fast line. When the complete line has only one curve in it, it is known as a simple curved line. If it curves in two directions, it is a compound-curved line. "Fast" compound-curved lines (Fig. 18) suggest waves, paths of smoke, silk flowing in the breeze or low-lying cloud formations. "Slow" compound-curved lines present the idea of writhing serpents, snarled fishing lines, or a map of tortuous country roads (Fig. 19).

What is meant by "rhythmical lines"? Rhythm implies more than one thing. The straight line by itself has no rhythm, but a

Fig. 22. Wavy lines can produce a rather sentimental look as shown by this peacock feather motif taken from a vase designed in 1900.

number of straight lines might be rhythmically related. Several curved lines, whether simple or compound, might also be grouped rhythmically producing a subtle relationship or unity. Fig. 20. What determines this rhythm is mainly a matter of individual feeling. No formula can be presented. Explore situations in nature, such as movement in tall waving grasses, or strata in rock formations. If these give you a pleasant sensation, make a mental note of them, or better still, jot them down in your notebook with the intention of developing them later. There is a kind of rhythmical order as one line leads into another—one line "goes with" (not parallel to) another, and so on.

It would appear that lines are not always curved and rarely straight in nature; some would be more correctly labeled "bent." The bent line has some straight parts to it and a variety of rounded corners, some acute, some obtuse. Fig. 21. Bent lines are more organic in character—more expressive—than mechanical compass curves. In fact, there is considerable difference between curved and bent lines; each will give an entirely different character to a design. Too many curved lines often give an effect of "sweetness" especially if the curved line approaches an "S" curve. In the Art Nouveau period, at the turn of the century, the curved wavy lines were used so much that a rather sentimental character and "slithery" appearance became associated with art of that time. One recalls blown glass flower vases and stained glass lamp shades, furniture, and even interior architecture of the period which clearly illustrated the designer's preoccupation with the wavy and curved lines. Fig. 22.

The character of line itself is related to economic, social, or cultural developments. People today do not react to pretty sentimental curves as they did in 1900 and consequently there is more variation of line; more angular, bent, shaded, and broken lines are used in all forms of contemporary design.

A shaded line (Fig. 24), or a line which has different thicknesses, has many uses for the designer. A shaded line tends to disappear where it is thin and come forward where it is thick, enabling the

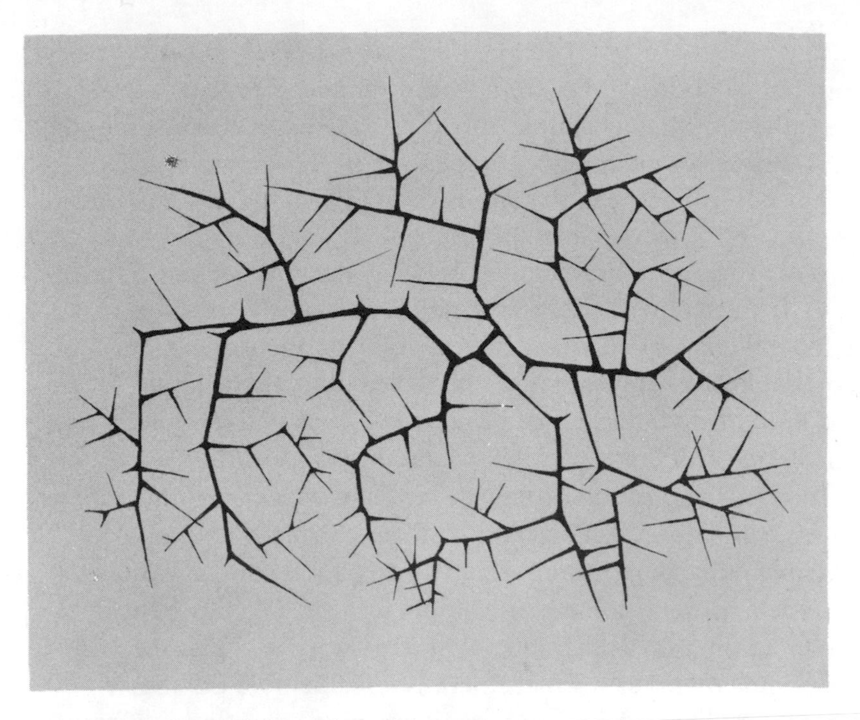

Fig. 23. In the tumbleweed the line continues, even though the extruded points confuse the main direction of the line.

Fig. 24. A shaded line seems to come forward and go back.

Manuscript Writing
Manuscript Writing
Manuscript Writing
Manuscript Writing
and ILLUMINATING
Illuminating
by Sister Michaeline
SCRIBE...

Writing Script

Fig. 25. Sister Michaeline. In manuscript writing, imagination is an asset—the capital "M" has three variations, but it is skillfully controlled. The line is not completely free, as the manuscript pen has its limitations. Preconceived formality denies complete freedom of line in any form of calligraphy.

Fig. 26. Character and freedom resulted when the student used a twisting motion with sticks dipped in tempera paint.

artist to stress emphasis in the design. This line could also have points sticking out from it as a twig from a thorn bush with its long sharp briars. The tumbleweed found in the desert portrays this character with its extruded points and shaded lines. Fig. 23. Try some experiments with the brush held vertically to the paper. By applying different pressures, or by dragging the brush, a free sensitive quality is attained. One might study the exquisite calligraphic pen and brush work of the East Indian designs or those found in contemporary manuscript writing (Fig. 25). This type of line is shaded in a formalized manner, and is the result of highly trained skills. Our previous line designs mentioned above showed more freedom and less formality.

Lastly, there is the kind of line which is made up of overlapping or separate parts. This we will call a "textured" or "broken" line. Lines of this type bring out the very character for which we are searching, a sense of freedom and looseness rather than sleekness and superficiality. Do not put any limitations on the instrument or tool used. Try some of these experiments: The cross section of a small piece of synthetic sponge dipped in ink or tempera and played along in a moving line, toothpicks and small slivers of wood held lengthwise and used as a printing tool to create overlapping lines, holding the toothpick at one end while moving the other end, giving small fanlike shapes (Fig. 26); dragging a pocket comb across the paper with tempera or ink on it; dribbling with strings soaked in tempera paint, and so on. These lines need not be thought of merely as exercises. Plan to adapt them to one of the specific problems we are going to undertake. As original ideas evolve, the designer finds that each type of line expresses something to him (Fig. 27): nervousness, speed, quietness, drapery, textured bark, or merely sketchy lines which are used to create an atmospheric quality.

Fig. 27. Winds give the feeling of unrest and nervousness.

SHAPE

The spot and the line exist as elements in design. But if the line touches itself then it encloses an area or shape which is the third basic element. If you turn to the dictionary and look at the definitions for "shape," "area," "mass," and "size," you will find much duplication in the meanings given and possibly become quite confused. Yet the artist makes everyday use of these terms but perhaps gives them special meaning. Let us say that by speaking of "shape" an artist is usually referring to contour, especially when it describes a flat or two-dimensional object. "Area" is a quantitative term quite different from "shape." "Area" concerns the number of square inches within the two-dimensional shape; it is a tract or portion of any given surface. "Mass" is a term given to describe the extent of volume or bulk, yet one often hears the words "mass" and "area" used synonymously. To clarify this point let us make the following statement: "Area" is always used to describe a two-dimensional object. "Mass," on the other hand, may be used to describe a two-dimensional or three-dimensional object. Here the designer *must* understand what he is talking about. Underlying the study of basic design is the problem of manipulating, placing, and juxtaposing shapes, lines, and spots. The artist spends a lifetime with such elements, transfigured, of course, by his desire to express his meaning and message through the interpretation of these elements.

We have discussed straight, curved, bent, and broken lines. We could systematically create shapes whose contours were restricted to each of these types of lines. There are times when we are making a purely geometric kind of design, for instance when the style might demand shapes composed entirely of straight line contours. Fig. 28. In spite of this restriction of mechanically straight contours there is no reason to feel that the shape loses interest. It depends on the proportion and selection of these straight con-

Fig. 28. Straight line contour.

Fig. 29. Curved line contour.

Fig. 30. Bent line contour.

Fig. 31. Negative and positive areas.

Fig. 32. Simplicity, meaning, emphasis, balance, rhythm.

Fig. 33. Unrelated details lose "design meaning."

Fig. 34. Even distribution lacks "emphasis."

Fig. 35. With both contour and accents stressing one direction the shape seems "out of balance."

Fig. 36. Confusion in direction and lack of inner structure lose the sense of "rhythm."

tours. Similarly a shape might have contours of curved lines (Fig. 29), bent lines (Fig. 30), or a combination of all types of lines.

There may be a hole or holes in the shape, or a chunk or bite may be taken away from the edge. This part which is deleted from the original shape is known as a "negative shape." Fig. 31. Do not overlook the importance of studying negative as well as positive shapes. The negative areas play a vital role, and are, in reality, more important than the positive parts. The space between the leaves silhouetted against a dark background actually creates more of a pattern than the leaves themselves. Fig. 159.

How does one discover a "good" shape? It is not necessarily the most currently fashionable shape. The shape that expresses your message is the one to search for. This more nearly approximates what is termed "a good shape" than one which you might trace from a design textbook. A good shape should be simple. Fig. 32. It should have a beginning and an ending; it should have *meaning, emphasis, balance,* and *rhythm.* Its contours should not have superfluous directions or bends where fewer will be more expressive. Remember that the word "*meaning*" implies "design meaning" not representational meaning. Fig. 33. A shape should be exquisite in a design sense, or have design potential, or be usable in a design. By "*emphasis*" (Fig. 34), be reminded of symphonic music, a fine poem, or a dance. There is inevitably a beginning statement, the development of that statement, the variations and deviations, and eventually the ending. Accents and dynamic build-up are placed near the beginning, near the end, or in the middle. By exactly the same token a well-designed shape can be emphasized in some part by the placement of accents, or by the adjustment of proportions. "*Balance*" (Fig. 35) is inescapable whether the shape we are concerned with is a purely abstract, or more literal shape. Many shapes in nature are in perfect balance, but just because we lackadaisically pick up a leaf, or a shell, or a piece of driftwood, bring it to the studio, and copy it, does not imply that we have a full knowledge of balance. The balance for us must come from within. We must be able to "feel" its balanced shape before we say, "it is balanced." *"Rhythms"* (Fig. 36) are within the shape, they are *"of it"* not *"on it."* Lines, folds, accents, and serrations may, in some cases, imply a certain rhythm, but the inner rhythms, the ones that are not seen, but sensed, the relations of dominant to subdominant proportions, the arithmetical relationships of points or protuberances, the subtle changes in color, texture, or markings, these constitute the inner rhythms.

If it were only a matter of analyzing each shape and applying some of the above rules, all would be quite simple. But it is

Fig. 37. Robert Motherwell, "Pancho Villa, Dead or Alive." This design has meaning, emphasis, balance, and rhythm. These factors, not always obvious, are instinctively felt by the artist.

Fig. 38. Mauricio Aguilar, "Fish." The subtlety of the design depends entirely on the artist's sensitivity to position and his arrangement of spots of the same size, shape, and direction.

doubtful if any truly creative artist ever approaches the problem in this way. There are times when the solution to a design problem *is* based on a rule even though most artists deny it, but the student should realize that such qualities as *rhythm, balance, proportion, emphasis, simplicity,* and so on, are not academic man-made rules at all. They are universal laws, not rules. They are related to the forces of the universe, and are useful in solving the designer's problems. Artists must feel these forces but not display them obviously. Nothing could be less desirable than a piece of art work which is too perfect. This would leave no room for ambiguities or further exploration. It is only the imperfections and the unexpected that make art what it is. Fig. 37.

❦ CHAPTER II

DESIGN ELEMENTS COMBINED

Grouping of spots, lines, and shapes

LET'S take a handful of nails we might buy in any hardware store and drop them on the floor. As we look at these nails we may or may not see something which attracts us about the arrangement. If everyone felt that the nails were arranged attractively we would have little need for further discussion. But fortunately, all do not feel the same way about the accidental grouping. Fig. 39. Some would like to rearrange the positions to their own satisfaction. One person might be an orderly person who would prefer neat parallel groups. Fig. 40. Another, a musician, would visualize an arrangement of the nails which, to him, symbolized a song or a dance. Fig. 41. A farmer, perhaps, might see lines which represented growth, Fig. 42, and so on. Each person who arranges the nails is expressing his own design ideas.

In order for us to say that one straight line is related to (has something to do with) another, let us first have one line going in the same direction as the other. Fig. 43. This involves the universal principle of parallelism and because we can say "this goes in the same direction as that," the design shows *that kind* of relationship. Our lines which are parallel may be thick or thin; they may be long or short; they may also be far apart, near to-

Fig. 39

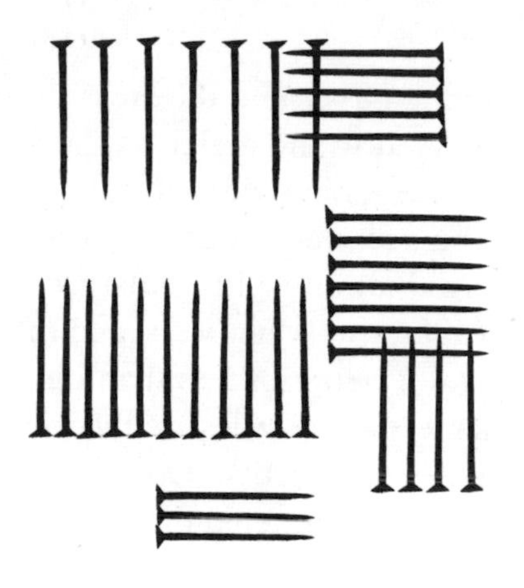

Fig. 40

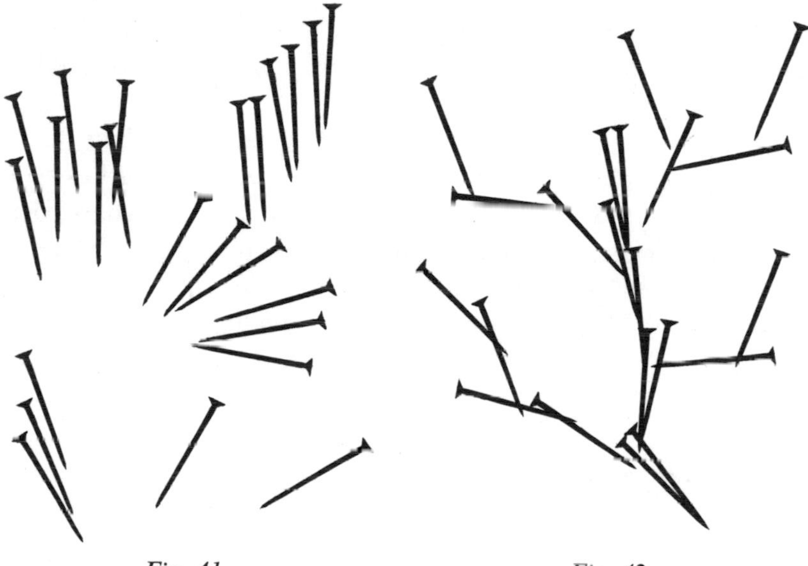

Fig. 41

Fig. 42

gether, touching, or overlapping. They may be used as single items or be grouped in such a way to form a heavy line from many fine ones. With this one relationship alone, the opportunity for variety is endless, especially since we are working on a sheet of white paper and the areas of white paper which are left become as vital to the design as the lines themselves.

We, as individuals, can feel that what we do is our own. No one need judge our arrangement but ourselves. Our sense of discrimination will be enlarged as soon as we make more than one trial. And when we see another artist's arrangement we either like it better or less than our own because it is not the same. In spite of any rules or theories, our basis for evaluation can be purely subjective. Does the design make us want to dance or to rest, is it cluttered or monotonous in its spacing, does it hold our interest or fail to communicate, or does it merely seem to be a group of lines and nothing more?

The second relationship is one in which lines go in exactly the opposite directions. Fig. 44. Such an arrangement embodies another principle known as "opposition." If one can say, "this line goes in the opposite direction from that line," it therefore has this kind of a relationship.

Of more concern to us than the mere fact of calling this a "principle of design" is the universal law which underlies such opposing lines. Think of the many situations in everyday existence which exemplify this thought. The horizon line is in direct contrast or at right angles to upright man, trees, flowers, and the great geysers. Confucius recognized this law when he spent a full day in deep contemplation and arrived at the philosophical fact

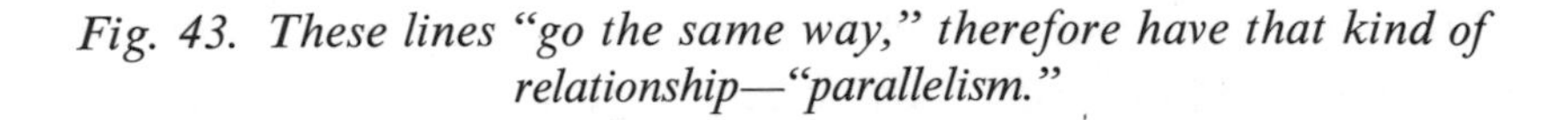

Fig. 43. These lines "go the same way," therefore have that kind of relationship—"parallelism."

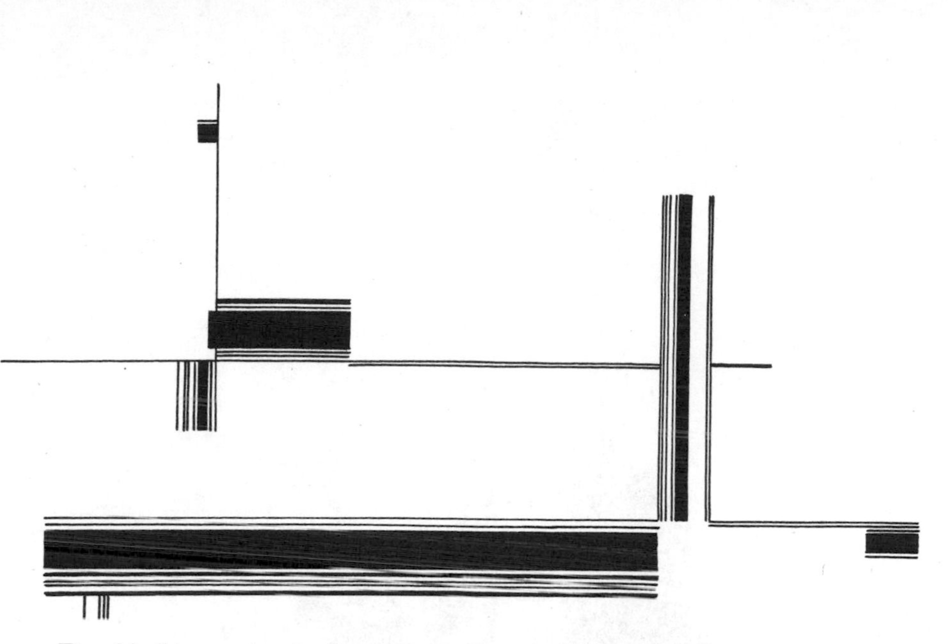

Fig. 44. Lines going in the opposite direction have a relationship, which is based on one of the universal laws—"opposition."

that "trees grow upright." We are so accustomed to these natural phenomena that we do not search for their deeper meanings. But the designer must sense these forces in nature and make use of them in composing. Often a design embodies a complex series of opposing lines, each stress resolving the stress in another part of the picture. Telephone poles, standards for bridges, and piles upon which a wharf is built could be thought of as man's persistent expression of the same rule. Our whole attitude about design might be based on the exploration of some simple principle. If we can make use of these simple principles and still not have the design appear *contrived* we have probably arrived at a satisfying solution.

The theologian will tell us that the Christian symbol of two straight lines arranged in opposition has its connotations. The relation of this symbol to the human figure is self-evident, but there is another meaning—that of the vertical standard representing man's aspirations, and the horizontal line being symbolic of his earthly existence.

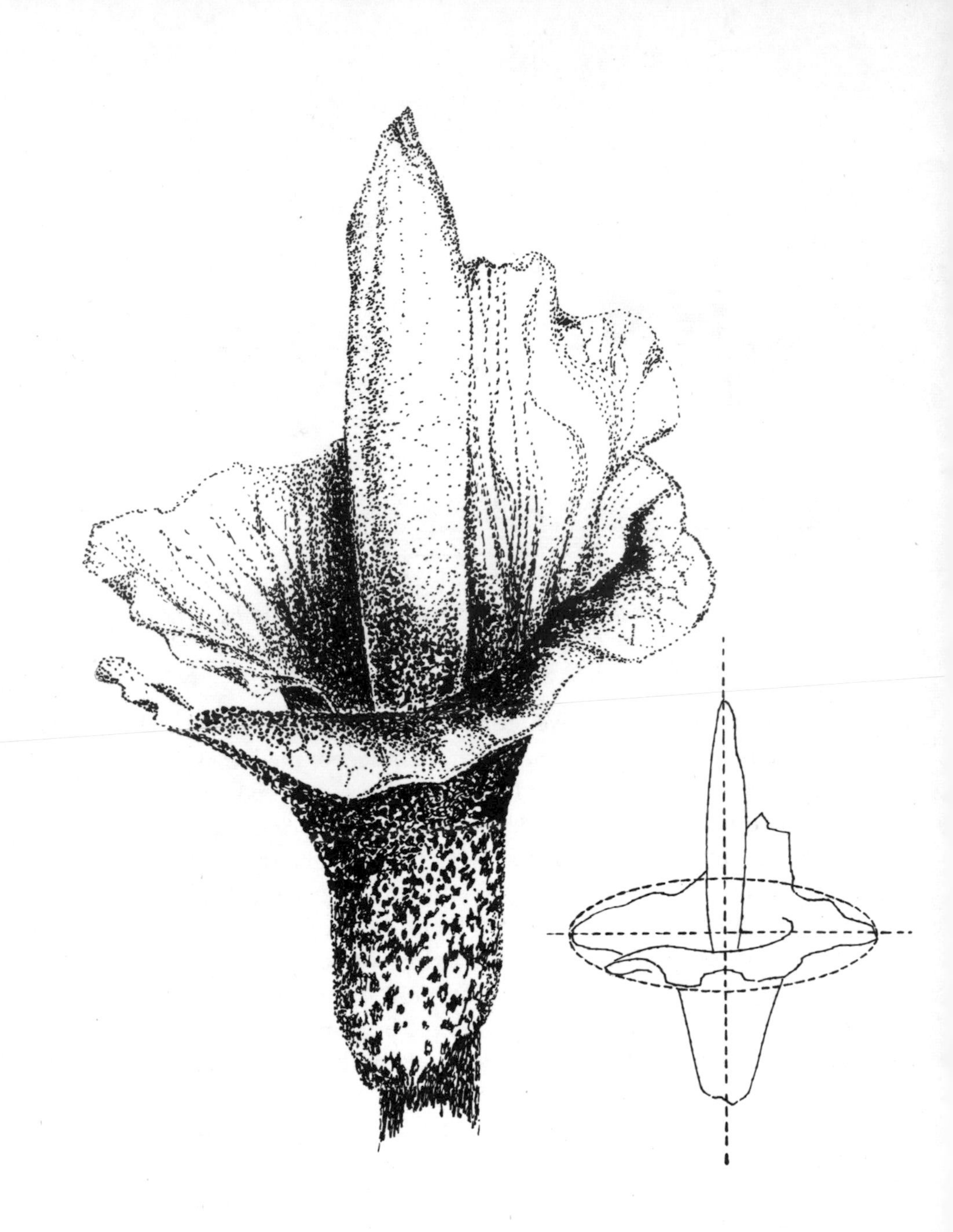

Fig. 45. Opposition is expressed in many flowers by the vertical pistil and the horizontal plane *of the petals or corolla.*

In the plant world vertical and horizontal opposition is clearly shown in almost every flower or plant growth. In a calla lily, jack-in-the-pulpit, or any member of the large arum family (Fig. 45), we have the bold and conspicuous flare of the corolla or horizontal plane of the flower in direct contrast to the tongue or pistil part which points straight upward. Opposition involves

Fig. 46. Kenneth F. Bates, "Hen and Rooster," enamel. The artist's answer, when he incorporates two unlike elements in the same design—such as the above "male and female" or the frontispiece, "large and small"—rests entirely on two vital principles: Rhythm (position of the major axes) and Balance (distribution of weights, stresses, color interests, etc.).

the law of balance. Nature relates forces which are inevitably in balance. This is not always a symmetric balance, but a balance of two unlike objects which offers a more challenging design problem. Fig. 46 and Frontispiece. The artist is essentially concerned with irregularity rather than regularity, with the broken tempo rather than the mechanical balance.

The principle of "two" predominates in life. Primitive man thought in terms of duality (Fig. 47): God and man; heaven and earth; the strong and the weak; two-headed deities; and two-headed serpents. Extremely brilliant colors and patterns occur on a male duck, peacock, or male cardinal, but to complete the balance of inequalities we find the female subdued in color and smaller in stature. The designer should concern himself with plus and minus, large and small, dull and bright. Listen to the recurrence of a musical motif in any fine symphony. There is repetition of the motif but invariably with some change, either louder, softer, differently instrumented or interpreted.

Fig. 47. Primitive man often thought in terms of duality, but introduced dissimilarities such as those shown in the eyes and backbone.

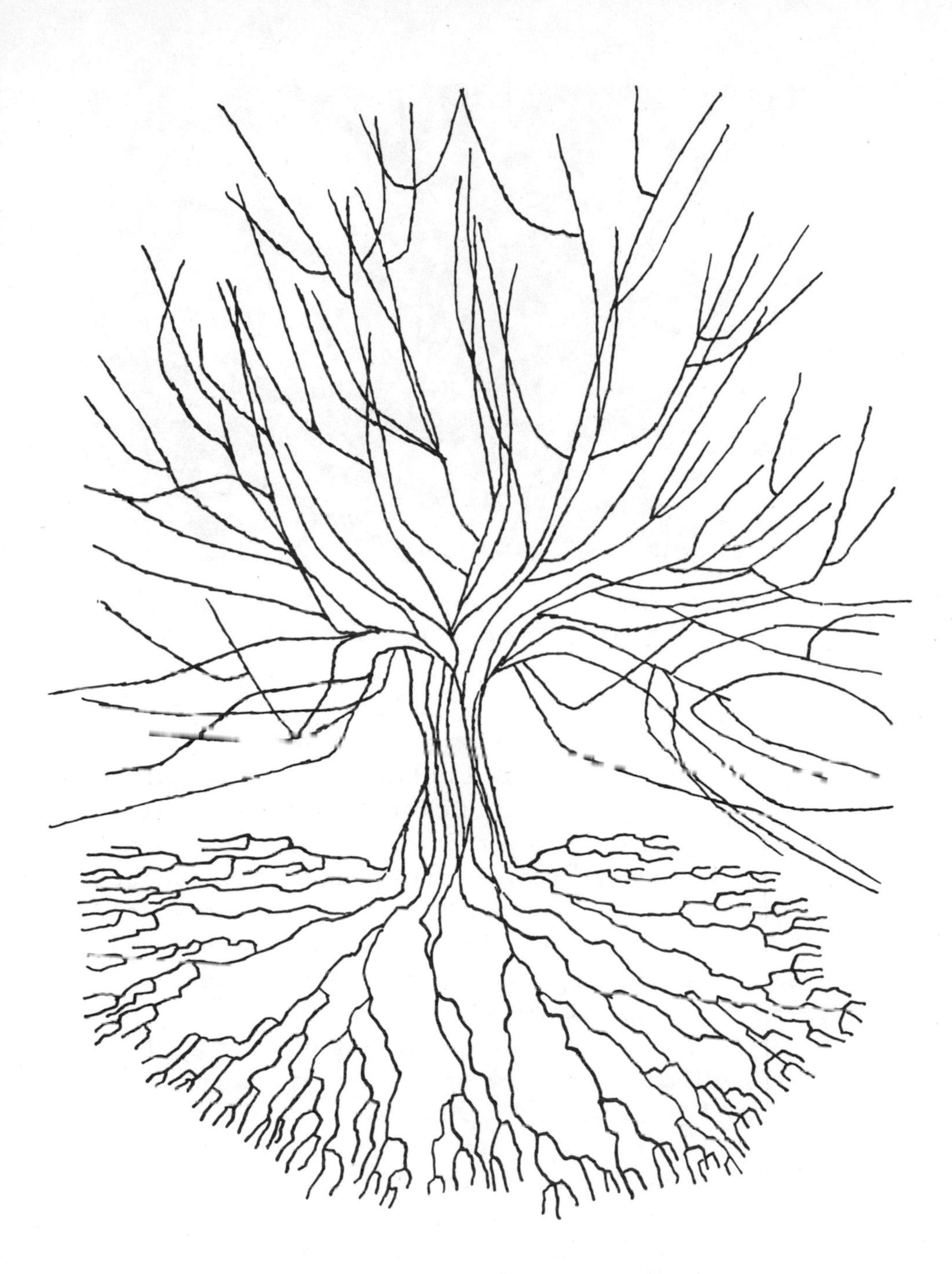

Fig. 48. A seed gives rise to radiation in two directions.

Fig. 49. Strong and thin, in and out, depth and rhythm—this combination of lines has considerable emotional impact.

Another relationship or principle is that of "radiation." Straight, curved, bent, shaded, or broken lines may be arranged so that they appear to start from one given point, sometimes visible (that is, on the paper) or from an unseen point (off the paper). Life constantly starts from a point and fans outward in all directions. A seed is planted—roots fan downward from this point, and stems, twigs, or branches spread upward. Here is a clearly defined example of radiation in two directions with the seed as a starting point. Fig. 48.

In trying some examples of radiating lines, do not be too obvious. There may be a "feeling" of radiation which is suggested but not shown. There may be within the composition many starting points, some outside of the page and some within it.

We have discussed three basic ways in which lines are related. These are: going in the same direction (parallelism), going in opposite directions (opposition), and starting from a common point (radiation). These are associated with the laws which represent perfection in order, as opposed to chaos. But what about arrangements of lines which are not based on any of these laws? These also have interest and meaning to the designer. Too close an adherence to the rules in design produces an unimaginative and sterile quality. Lines might go "in any direction" but still have a fascinating sense of order. Our experimentation with arrangement of lines should certainly include this last classification. Fig. 49.

The arrangements we make are either pleasing or not. An explanation is unnecessary. If art can be explained, it is not art. If the lines create a feeling of restfulness, of excitement, of dancing, or of wind blowing, that is enough. The artist's reason is that he is expressing an *idea* of something. After experimentation with abstract spots, lines, and shapes comes the need for research and inspiration. Otherwise we may feel that we are trying to take something out of our heads when little has been put into them. By exposing our minds to this preliminary study of the basic laws of nature we have some basis for using inspiration when it comes to us.

It is less difficult to combine any line with any shape than to combine a given line with a given shape. This means that a particular line does not always go with a particular shape. Let us start then with a shape which we have painted in silhouette with the brush. Suppose the shape is one which is not symmetric. It has a long and a short axis, and more than one point or protuberance. Now our problem is to find one line which will be well designed with this one shape. Fig. 50. Reconsider our discussion of the relationship between different lines, and see if the same principles do not apply here. Mere intellectualizing about the line is of little value. A line is not "found" by thinking about it! It is "found" by trying to draw it. The process is purely empirical, a matter of trial and error. No one today particularly cares whether or not the first line an artist puts down will become his final choice. This point of view is outmoded. Freedom in design is a matter of searching, and the result of many trials—of developing a keen sense of discrimination and tasteful selection. The final result may give the impression of having been done quickly and easily, but the number of preparatory sketches is as much the work of the artist as the number of hours of practice a pianist needs to memorize a concerto is the work of a musician.

This line we are searching for, which is related to the shape, may be thought of in many ways. It may be a line which is parallel to the shape in one of two ways. It could be parallel to the contour; it might cross the shape or not; it could be parallel to the long or short axis of the shape, whether that axis is seen or not. Fig. 51.

The line might go entirely in the opposite direction from the way the shape "goes." The shape "goes" in the direction of its long axis. These two elements—the line and the shape—might appear to radiate from a focal point. The focal point does not have to be within our picture; it may equally well be an imaginary point outside the picture.

Fig. 50. A challenging problem is to combine one line with one shape—a completeness that is satisfying without being obvious.

Fig. 51. The line is parallel to the contour of the shape at the upper left, but opposes the long axis elsewhere.

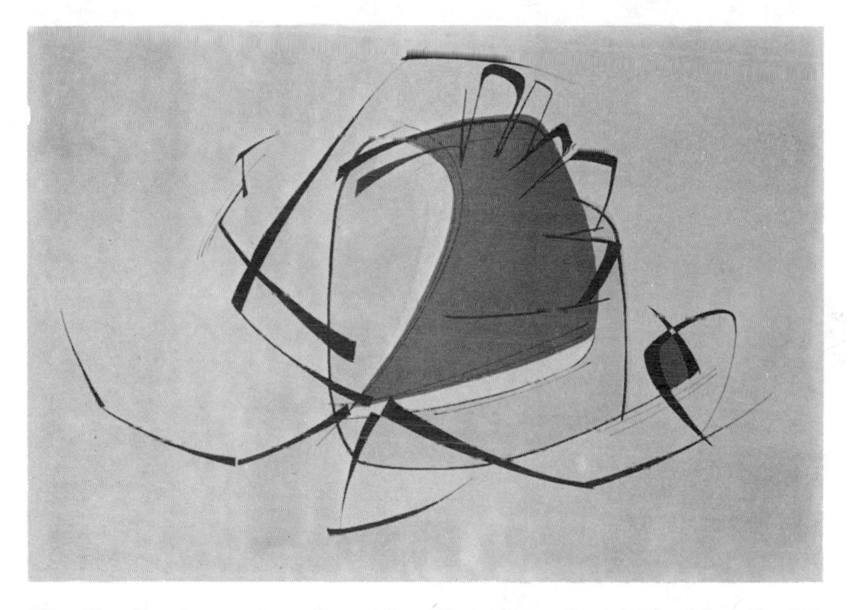

Fig. 52. An abstraction of a spider. These lines were evolved by allowing the brush to move freely in and out and around the shape.

Suppose after basing our trials on these principles we approach the problem in a less tangible manner. Move the pencil or brush freely in and out and around the shape. Fig. 52. We discover a line which holds our interest. This line, perhaps a shaggy, shaded, or compound line, has a pleasing effect to *us*.

As soon as we have accomplished this experimentation which

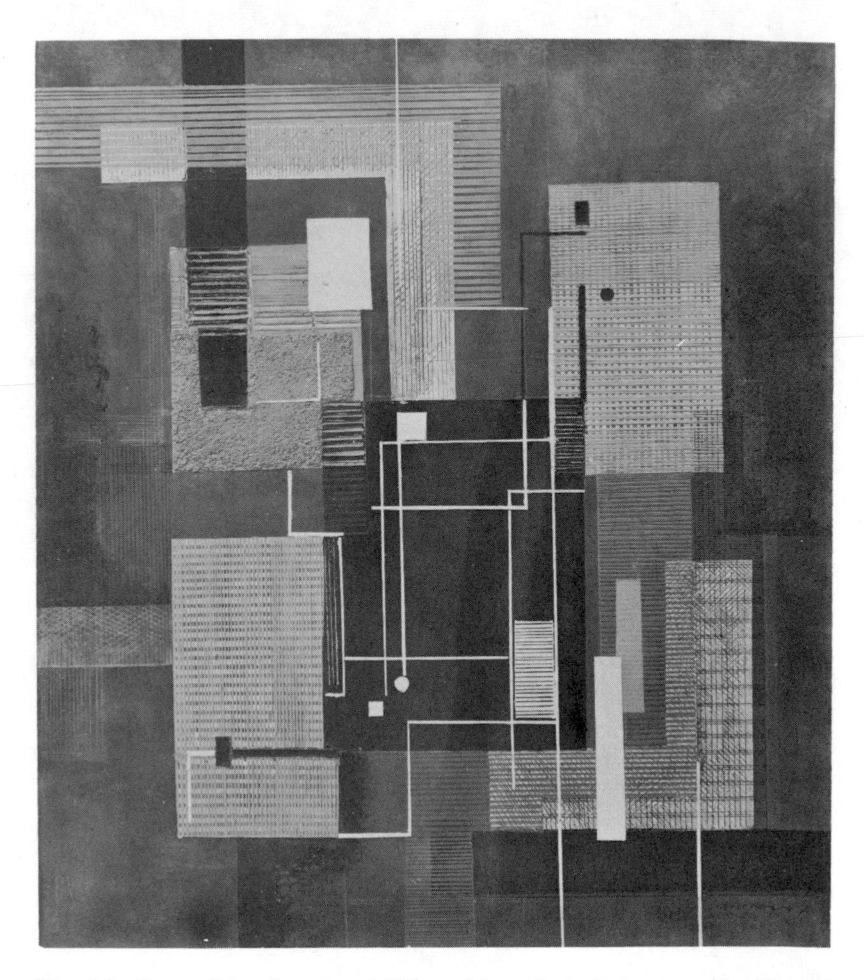

Fig. 53. Irene Rice Pereira, "White Lines." A design may be "built" much as an architect builds a structure.

is a vital step in the process of creating a design, we are ready to continue the process. May we not combine two lines with one shape, two lines with two shapes, and so on? Each additional part which we add to the composition should enhance what has gone before. In other words, we are "building" a design, much as an architect builds a structure. Perhaps we do not find an excuse for each part as the architect must, but still we feel in our own minds, that what we add to our original premise has some excuse for being. Fig. 53.

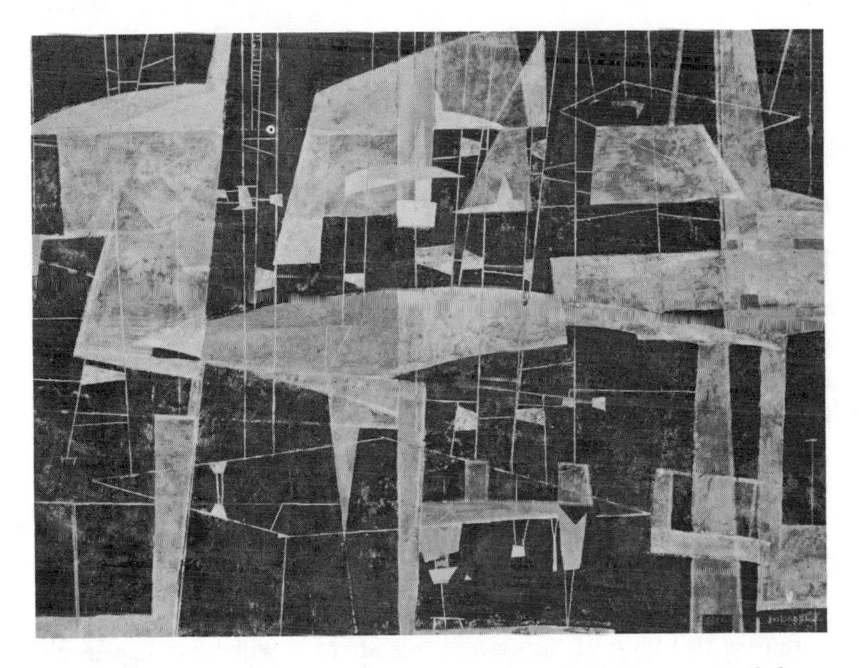

Fig. 54. A method of space filling, making use of line, spot, and shape, creates "allover texture." No particular area is emphasized.

CHAPTER III

DESIGN IN TEXTILES, WEAVING, AND WRAPPING PAPER

The motif, repeat of motif

SO FAR in our study of design we have concentrated upon theory, searching, as much as possible, for instances in life about us where those theories are revealed. Now, as we continue to explore the underlying principles that make design what it is, let us take up more practical applications of these principles. The first practical problem will be that of textile designing, whose basic ideas may also be applied to something like wrapping paper (Fig. 55) or weaving (Fig. 56). This is not a "how-to-do-it" book, so that we shall not attempt to describe a technical process such as silk screen printing for a textile, weaving techniques, or block printing. This chapter explains how one goes about creating *a design for* textiles.

Before thinking of how an entire surface will be covered, we must extend our study of the spot, line, and mass to develop what is called a motif. This motif can then be duplicated or varied in its repetition to make a pattern or "field." "How to start" is sometimes a matter of personal preference. Some artists start to make a motif by considering the general outside contour of the whole. Whether it is going to be a long vertical motif, or whether it will take on the general appearance of a short and stubby area must

Fig. 55. An interesting pattern for Christmas wrapping paper.

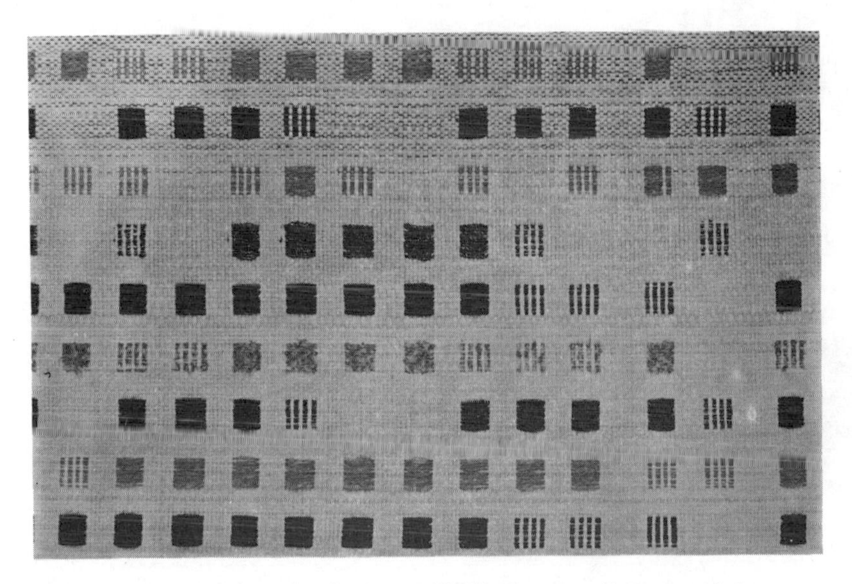

Fig. 56. Kay Sekimachi, "Woven Wall Hanging." Spots of the same size, shape, and direction but of different values.

Fig. 57. When starting a motif consider the general shape. Think and sketch in "squarish," "longish," or "roundish" terms.

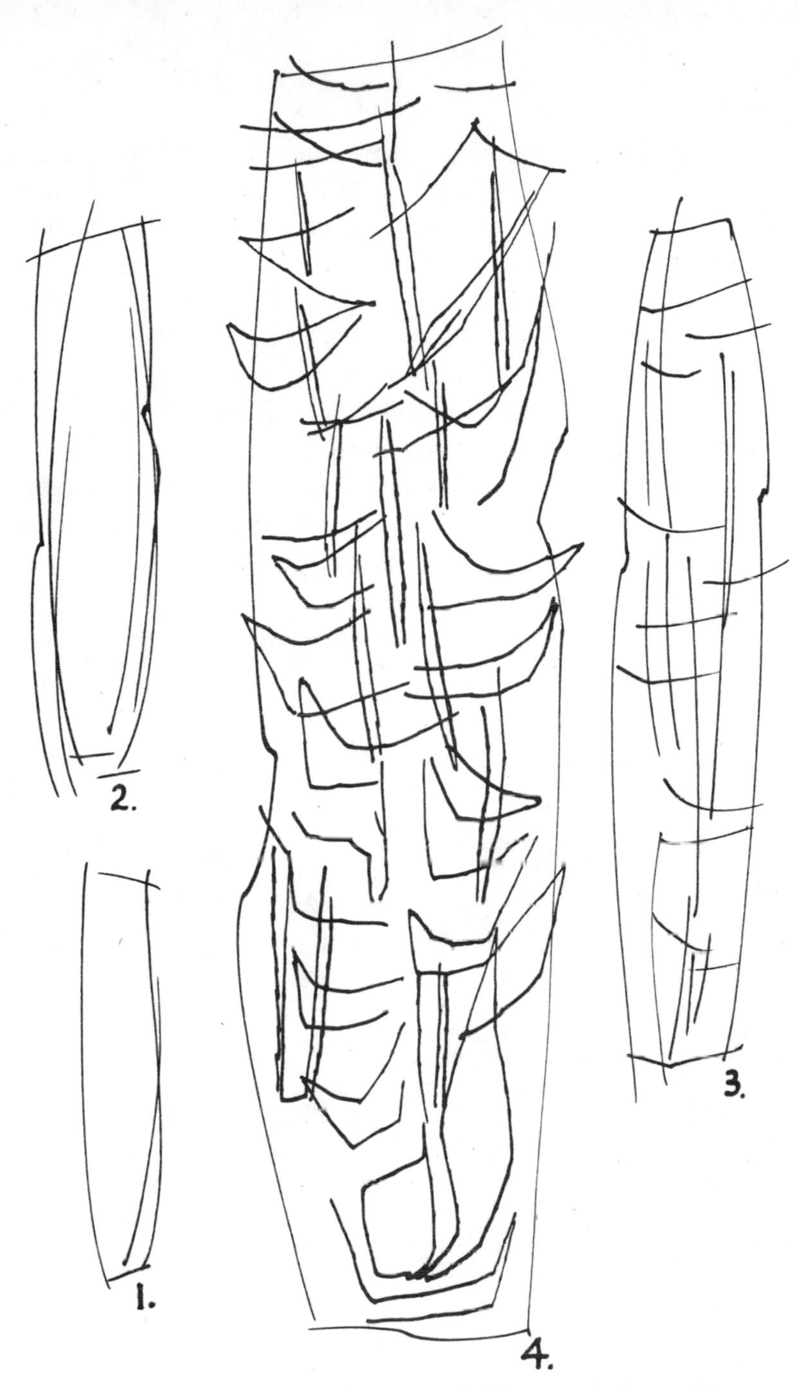

Fig. 58. "Thinking on paper" begins with (1) general shape, (2) major movement, (3) counter-movement, (4) development of the idea.

be decided at this point. Fig. 57. We must consider how the motif will be used, what its function will be in the larger scheme. Sketching the general idea of the mass of the motif by scribbling lines is recommended.

Many artists, in fact, begin their initial "thinking on paper" with what could be called a "doodle." Fig. 58. We may say that a "doodle" is "subconscious thinking on paper," rather than saying that "the artist is unconscious of what he puts on the paper." One may scribble away for hours and gain nothing, the last design having no more potential than the first one. This type of sketching constitutes an unconscious, or insensitive way of working. On the other hand, applying a certain amount of thinking, but at the same time allowing oneself to be free and fluent will show that each effort is an improvement on the preceding

Fig. 59. This nonobjective motif relies for its impact upon a subtle use of texture, dark upon light and light upon dark, spots with and without holes, and a sense of humor.

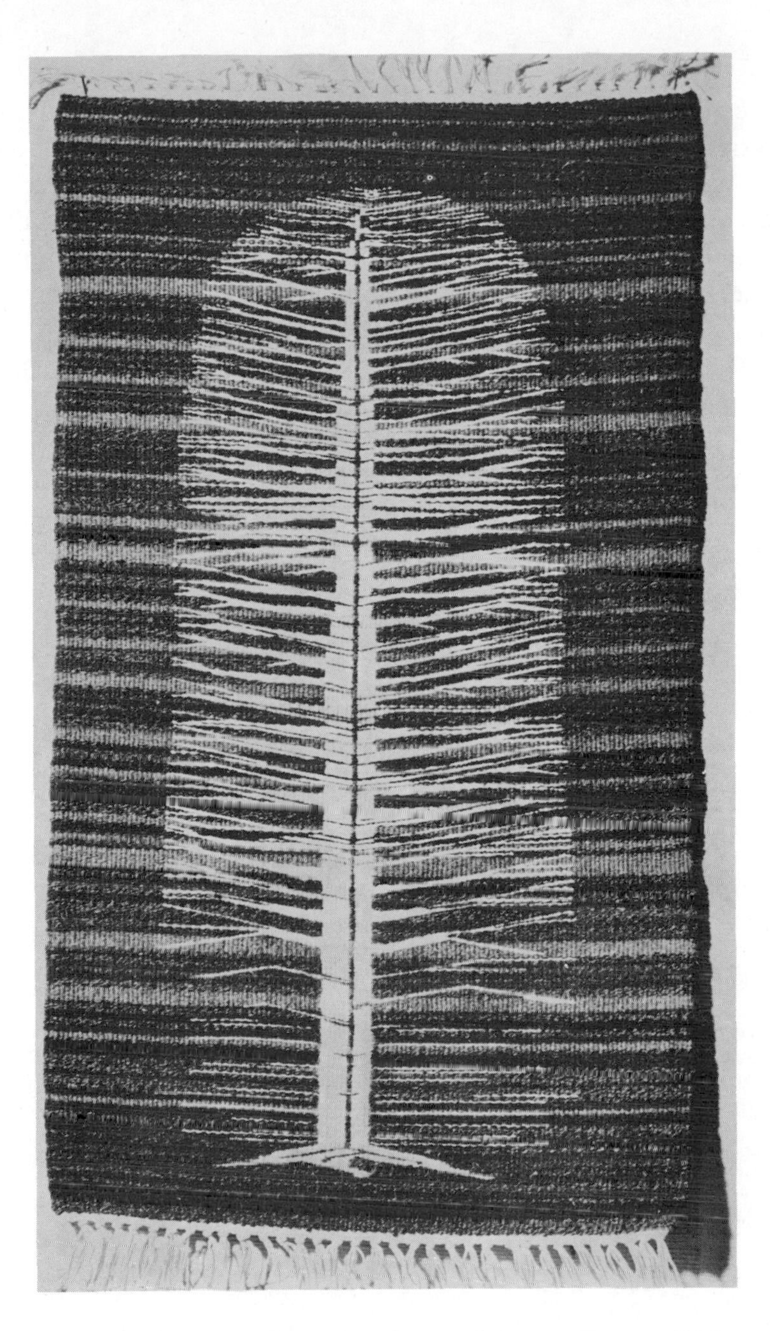

Fig. 60. Claribel McDaniel. "Wool and Cotton Tapestry." The rhythmical lines are both parallel and opposite to the long axis.

one. There is no guarantee that the continued "redoing" of a design will improve it. Many times the first emotional doodle has a "flavor" which is difficult to recapture. Professional artists are often capable of creating juxtapositions of shapes and lines directly, but it is not essential that we arrive at a solution so quickly. Designing is a matter of exploration and research, with many trials needed before we will be able to select the best one.

The type of motif we are discussing here is one which will be composed of either abstract or nonobjective shapes and lines. The term "abstract" is loosely used by both artist and layman. In reference to the two classifications, "abstract" and "nonobjective," we must realize that a nonobjective motif could be called "abstract," but that an abstract design is not necessarily "nonobjective."

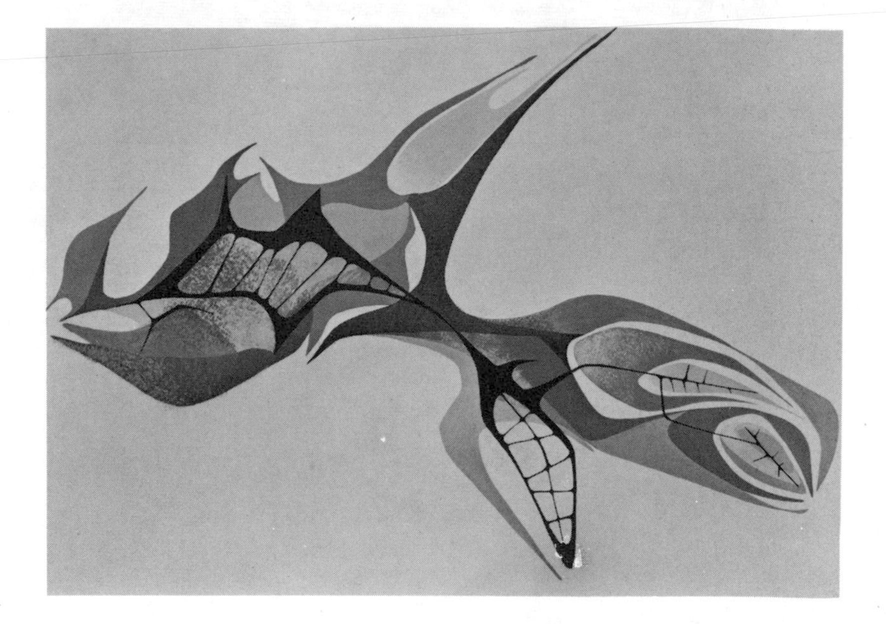

Fig. 61. Consistency unifies the whole motif. Notice the similar character of the points, the absence of purely geometric lines, etc.

Fig. 62. Repetition of the leaf and branch elements within the motif creates a convincing unity.

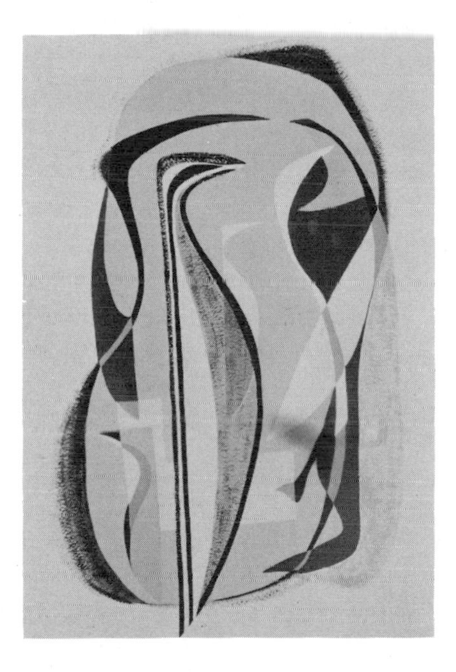

Fig. 63. An example of Gestalt Theory. The bird-like configuration occurs large, small, facing the left, facing the right, upside down, right side up, light on dark, and dark on light—at least twelve times.

The abstract motif usually has a subject which is "abstracted," even though no literal feature of this subject is evident. The nonobjective motif (Fig. 59), on the other hand, has no subject connotation whatsoever. As our approach to design so far has been primarily nonobjective (emphasizing design for design's sake) let us consider this type of motif first.

After the general idea of the outside shape has been decided upon, we must search for the main rhythmical lines within the shape. It would be possible to think of rhythmical lines which went "the long way of the basic shape" (parallel to the long axis) or contrary to the shape (opposite to the long axis.) Fig. 60. Rhythmical lines might also spiral or radiate within the shape, or zigzag from top to bottom.

Repetition of parts of the motif within the whole is important. Fig. 61. But making *every* part of a motif entirely different from *every other* part is a fault. This could be said of children who color each part of the picture with another crayon until all the crayons have been used. The child is not always aware that one color can be distributed in various places. A suggestion of repetition of the elements making up the motif helps to effect a more symphonic unity. Fig. 62. The same holds true in regard to colors, values, character, and mood.

When the configuration which is found in one part of the motif recurs in another shape, size, or position somewhere else, this kind of unity is said to be representative of the Gestalt Theory, which implies that the arrangement of separate elements in a motif is so integrated that collectively they are made to appear as one unit. Fig. 63. These suggestions deal more with the intellectual than emotional aspect of designing. You should also consider how you *feel* about certain kinds of music, seasons, shapes, or colors. The intellectual and the emotional approach should go hand in hand. Either by itself produces weak results.

The areas within the general shape of a motif may be arrived at in many ways. In the original planning, areas which are most pleasing may be used to break up the shape of the whole motif,

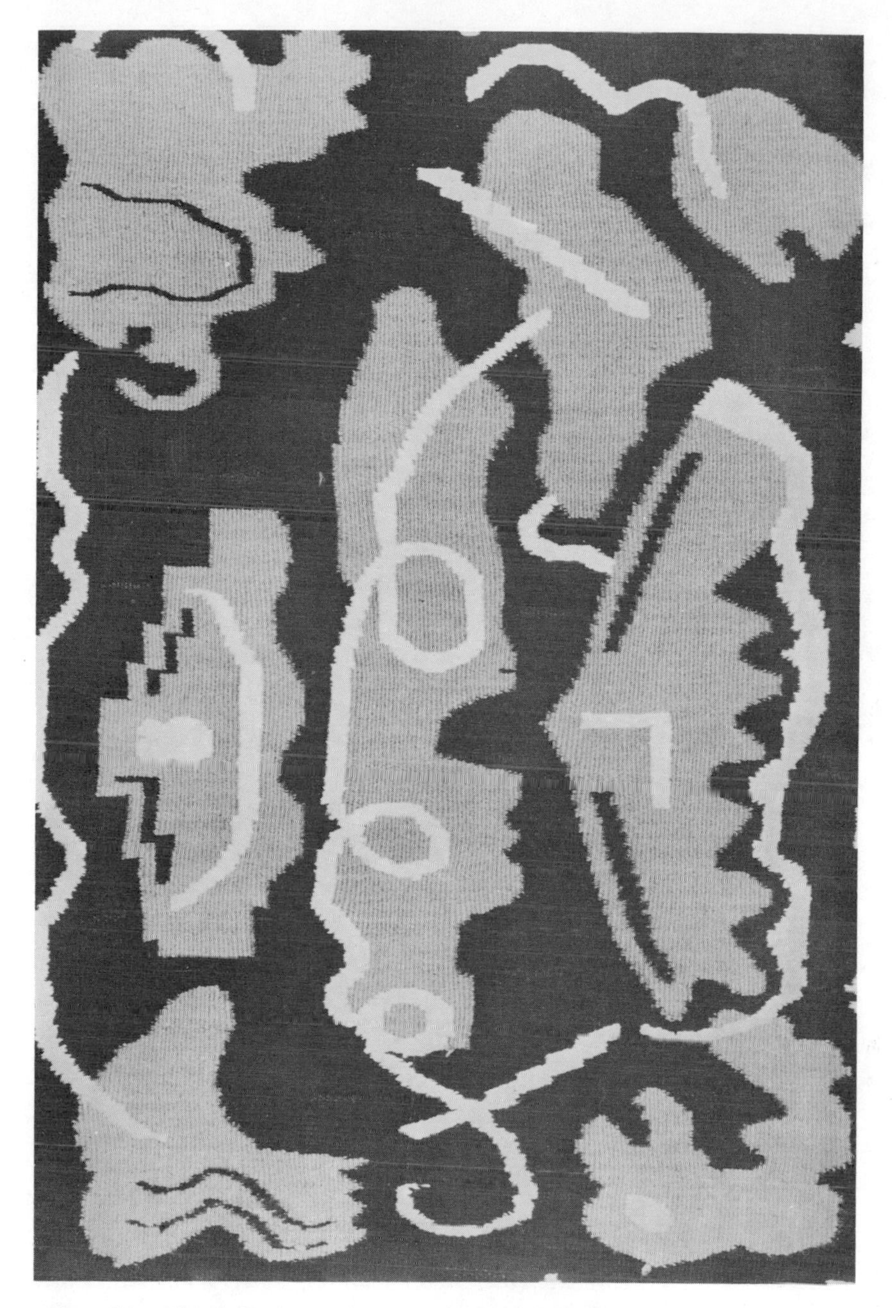

Fig. 64. Floyd Brewer, designer; Margreth Brewer, weaver; "Blue Rhythm." Overlapping lines add interest by "breaking up" the shapes.

Fig. 65. These pots are comparatively dull. The major dimension is primarily central; diameter of base and top are similar, etc.

Fig. 66. Viktor Schreckengost, "Composition, Pottery Forms." Each pottery shape is dramatized to suit the needs of the picture.

or separate shapes, worked out on tracing paper, may be moved about until they seem to "belong" to the whole motif. Overlapping lines sometimes help to break up the entire area. Fig. 64.

If these areas within the shape repeat the same dimensions (number of square inches) too often, there is bound to be monotony and lack of interest. This fault can easily be avoided by varying their shape, direction, and position as discussed in Chapter 1. (See also Fig. 143.) Dramatize wherever possible. Figs. 65, 66. Allow points to be sharper, large areas to be immense, small spots to be tiny, and so on. Simplification can also mean dramatization.

The motif, then, is constructed, drawn, colored, and rendered in a way which we hope will give pleasure to the viewer. We cannot expect to please others if we ourselves are dissatisfied. The motif is designed to be part of something—a part of something larger. It may be suited to a printed textile pattern (Fig. 69), to wrapping paper (Fig. 55), or to woven material (Fig. 60). It may be a group of many kinds of things which in some way or another appear to have aesthetic relationship. In any case there has to be conviction in the designer's mind for calling it a motif, before he conceives its possibilities for further use. The motif exists first as a unit by itself, secondly, repeated in a row, functioning as a border, and thirdly, row upon row, or in a field commonly called an "allover pattern." Fig. 67.

This allover pattern concerns us now for use as a textile design. In fact, we can review our analysis of the function of spots in design and apply it directly to the construction of a pattern. Transposing the motif for the spot we have the possibility of motifs that are far apart, near together, touching, and overlapping. It would be impossible to state how near together, or how far apart the motif should be. "Far apart" gives looseness and "breathing" to the pattern. "Near together" runs the danger of appearing overcrowded. Fig. 68. "Touching" creates a close-knit or compact character, but could also become unpleasant by the

Fig. 67. This plate shows a motif by itself, repeated in a row (border), and row upon row (field or pattern). Notice how, at a distance, the negative spaces form a diagonal pattern.

repetition of too many tangencies. The overlapping theory, which in textile printing is often obtained by superimposing other shapes and textures over the original design, can give us added richness. Fig. 69.

In a successful pattern the eye is made to travel *all over* the surface, not to focus too much in any one spot. This brings up the matter of function. If the pattern is to be used to wrap a gift or as upholstery material, it is not necessary that the design should "grow" one way. It should look as well one way up as another.

Scale is important. Always consider the distance from the observer when designing anything. This is function, but might also

Fig. 68. Indian rug, 17th century. Motifs near together can look crowded, but here a sumptuous surface enrichment is produced.

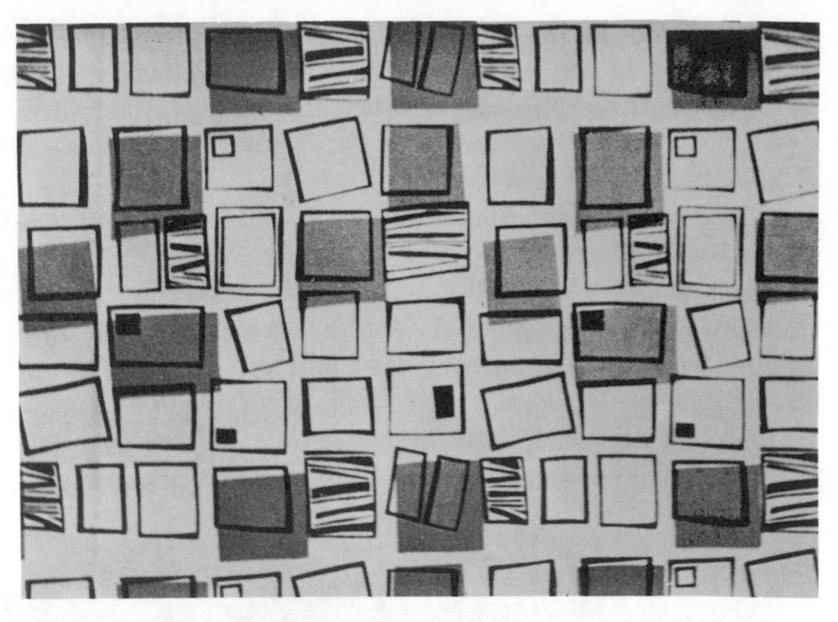

Fig. 69. Raul A. Coronel, "Printed Textile." "Overlapping," as studied in the first chapter, gives this pattern depth. This is an example of informal repeat.

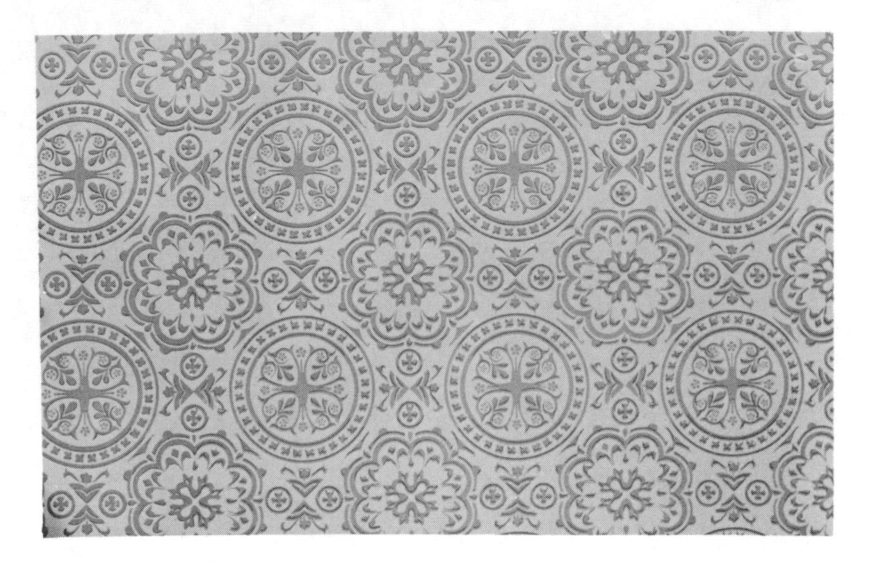

Fig. 70. Paul Riba. This wallpaper shows a formal repeat. The spacings are identical.

be called "common sense." A textile design which was meant for long drapes in a hotel lobby or as a room divider might have huge bold motifs where material for upholstery on a small intimate chair would make use of a close-knit motif in an entirely different scale. Sheer materials can accept more detailed motifs than coarser materials, and so on.

Methods of repeating the motifs are too numerous to list here completely. One may consider types of repeat patterns suggested by a conventional Coptic (Egyptian) textile or a recent contemporary wall hanging (Fig. 71). The endless ways in which the artist arrives at repetition in patterns are fascinating.

Let us say that all repeats may be classified as "formal" (Fig. 70), or "informal." However, in order to be of practical value our pattern must have some place where it "starts over," both horizontally and vertically. This area which eventually repeats

Fig. 71. Alice Adams, "Textile." Dramatic texture contrasts created by yarn and thread. Each bold spot is subtly placed.

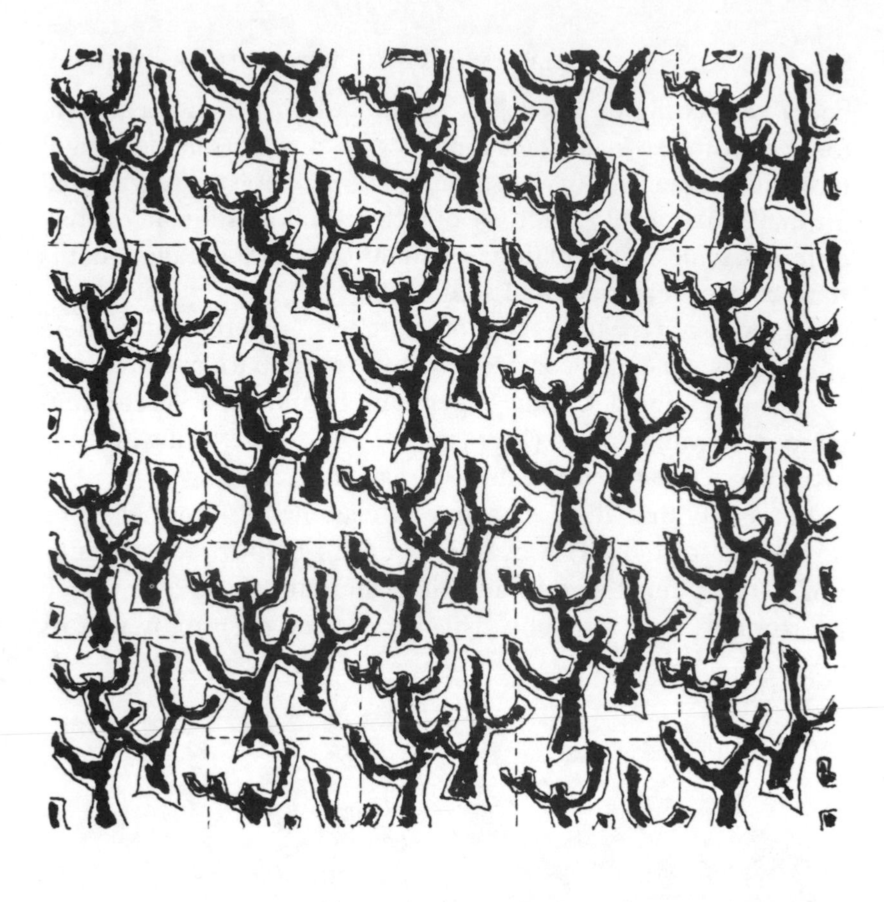

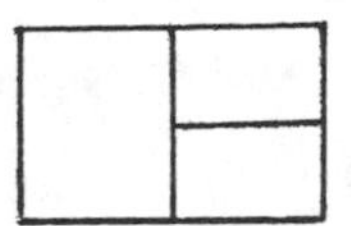

Fig. 72. The rectangular motif drops half its distance horizontally in each row. Diagram indicates unit of repeat.

below and across is known as the *unit of repeat.* Within this unit of repeat the motif may occur any number of times and in any kind of variation.

A few well-known ways in which the motif may be used within the unit of repeat are illustrated here. The structural lines used to lay out the pattern plan are naturally erased and employed only as a means of measuring, or (as in silk screen) registering, the placement of the motif.

1. Half-drop. Fig. 72. Lay out squares or rectangles which drop half their distance either vertically or horizontally. The motif is constructed within one of the areas and repeated. If the motif projects outside of the square or rectangular area it will tend

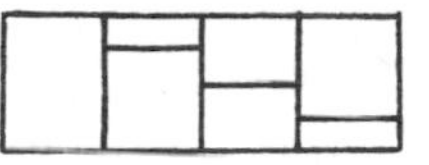

Fig. 73. The quarter-drop takes the width of four units and the depth of one to complete a unit of repeat, as the diagram indicates.

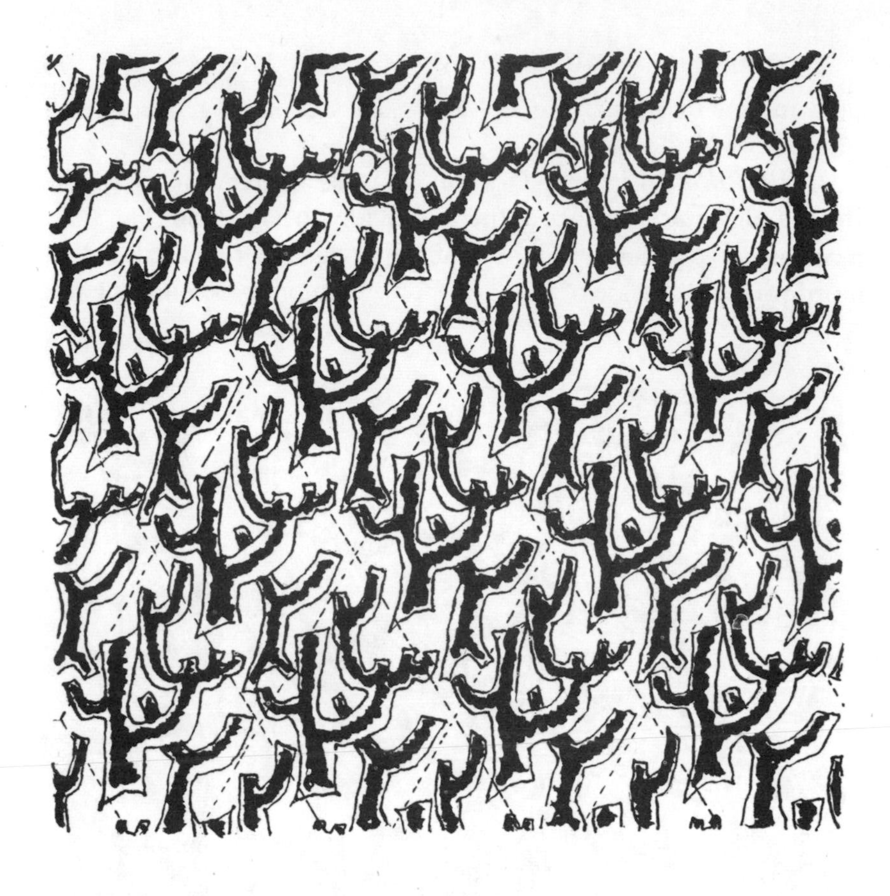

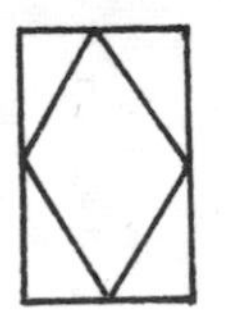

Fig. 74. The diamond repeat knits together. A full diamond and four quarters complete the unit of repeat, as the diagram shows.

to unify the pattern. This necessitates joining the lower right half of the rectangular motif to the upper left half. A slant of 45 degrees will result from this type of repeat.

2. *Quarter-drop.* Fig. 73. Quarter-drop, eighth-drop, etc., are accomplished as in the half-drop. It will be noticed that in these patterns a more gradual inclined movement results.

3. *Diamond repeat.* Fig. 74. The same motif occurs in every diamond. The upper right-hand side of the diamond is joined to the lower left, and the upper left to the lower right. Again by extending parts of the motif outside of the diamond and joining them in this way a more compact pattern is achieved and the

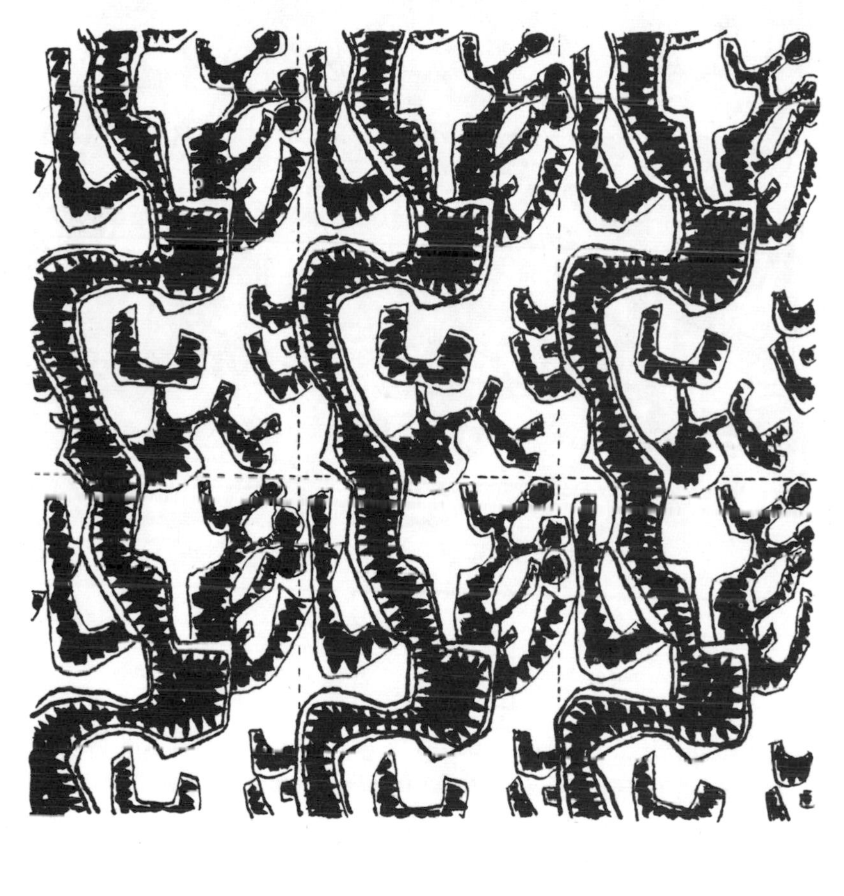

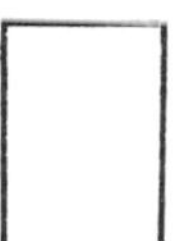

Fig. 75. In the parallel repeat the stem line is included in the rectangle which repeats above, below, and to the right and left.

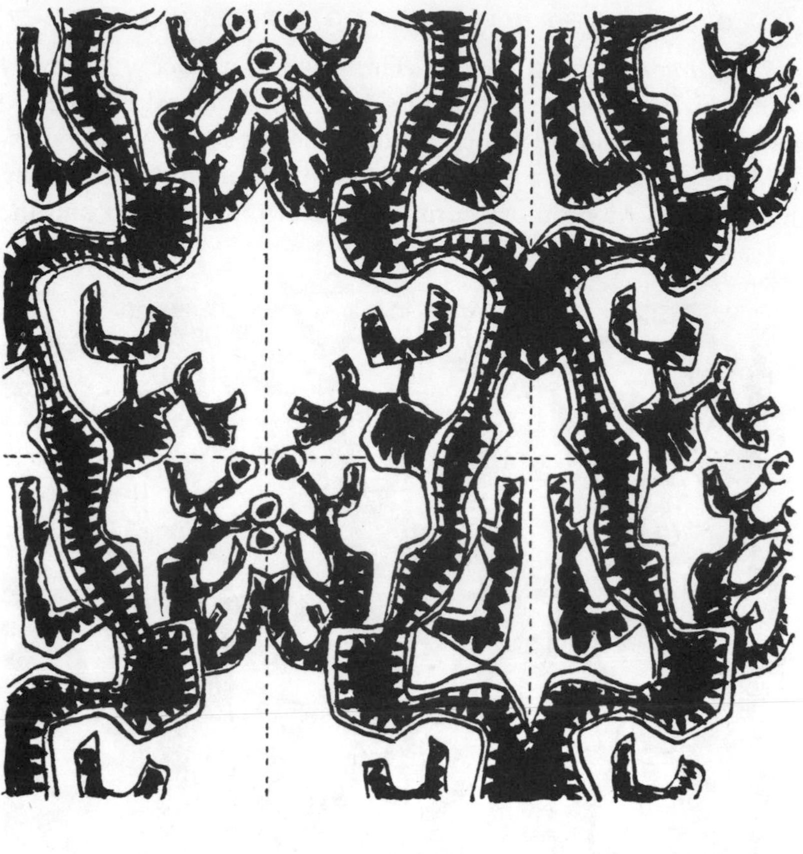

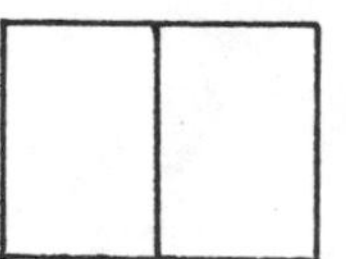

Fig. 76. Each rectangular motif is turned right for left in the horizontal row, resulting in a series of bisymmetric designs.

actual shape of the diamond is concealed. A diagonal movement is bound to result from the diamond repeat. A variation on the diamond repeat is gained by alternating the motif with another kind of motif, or by reversing it left for right in every other row.

4. *Parallel repeat.* Fig. 75. Here the structure line, or stem line, repeats directly across and parallel. From these parallel stem lines

any form of variation may occur. We must remember throughout these studies of pattern that the bottom edge of the entire unit of repeat must always be coincidental (joinable) to the top edge, and that the right and left edges of the unit join in the same way.

Fig. 77. Reversing black for white in alternating squares. Two squares down and two abreast complete the unit of repeat.

Fig. 78. This type of repeat can be explained simply (see p. 81), but is most mysterious if the system is not divulged. The unit of repeat is indicated in upper left-hand corner.

5. *Opposite repeat.* Fig. 76. The stem line, whether continuous or broken, is reversed left for right as it repeats across the pattern horizontally. What happens with and about these stem lines may be quite free and informal. The original intention of opposition is expressed as the pattern develops.

6. *Alternate repeat.* Fig. 77. The original layout may consist of squares, rectangles, or circles. By reversing the values in alternate squares (dark for light, and light for dark), the design is enriched. This device is many centuries old and can often be seen in woven textiles and block prints.

7. *The twenty-five square repeat.* Fig. 78. This type of repeat offers greater freedom in distribution of the motif. Lay out the unit of repeat in twenty-five squares. Choose any square in the first row horizontally and place your motif in it in any position.

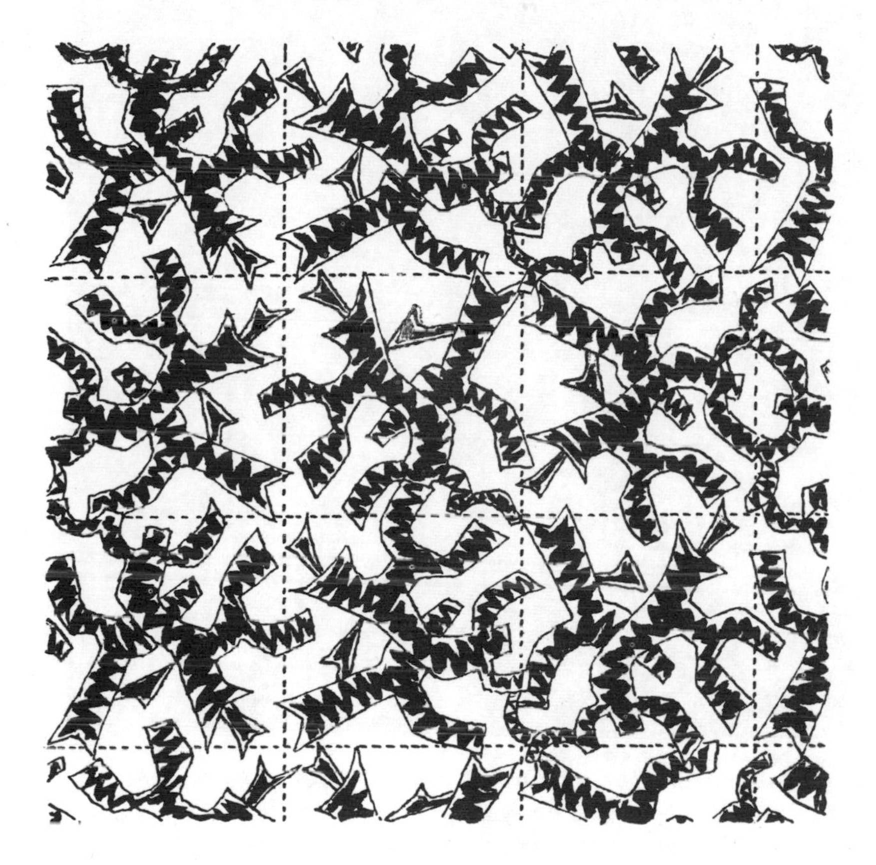

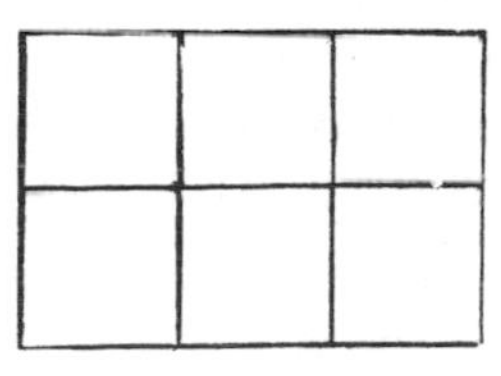

Fig. 79. The turning square repeat (see p. 84). The square turns in six different positions before repeating the unit.

Fig. 80. An example of a "turning square" repeat (the squares have been designated by dotted lines). It will be noticed that in every other row the squares take the same positions.

In the second row down, choose a square which is not directly below the first one chosen. Continue likewise in the third, fourth, and fifth rows horizontally. Repeat this same procedure with a smaller or alternate motif. The entire twenty-five squares are then repeated directly above and below, to the right and to the left. The result should be a free grouping of the motif in a variety of positions.

Fig. 81. This textile design appears to be entirely arbitrary and free, but when unfolded the material would show that the placing of the brush strokes is repeated in a large unit of repeat.

Fig. 82. English embroidery, James I period, 17th century. Study this carefully and you will find no two motifs exactly alike.

8. The turning square repeat. Figs. 79, 80. If this type of repeat is carried out correctly the end result should be completely mystifying and should defy detection as to how it was accomplished. Lay out the entire repeat in squares. Compose the motif on a separate piece of tracing paper in one of these squares. The design within the square is important. Allow the motif or motifs to be informally placed (not in the center and not parallel to the edge of the square). Also allow the shapes to project out of the square to some extent. We will now formulate a series of positions *on* the square layout being sure that the four points of our tracing paper square are placed directly on the four points of the layout squares. It will be observed that there are four choices for positions (original, quarter turn, half turn, and three-quarter turn), and by turning our tracing paper model upside down, we gain

Fig. 83. "La Fin des Moissons," a tapestry from original design by Maurice André. The Aubusson tapestry weavers in France have reproduced textile designs by famous contemporary artists.

four more positions. From these eight choices we merely decide upon a system of positions which pleases us most, and continue to trace into the square layout. As the design projects out of the square it can either overlap or go under the design next to it. This knits our pattern together giving a completely informal appearance. The entire unit of repeat consisting of two horizontal rows is then joined to the next one as in all patterns.

9. Scattered repeat. Lastly there is a kind of repeat which is often seen, and needs little explanation. In this type of repeat, where a fairly large unit is chosen without regard for any formal or systematized placing of the motif, we merely scatter it arbitrarily. Figs. 81, 82. The unit is then repeated in the usual way. All that is necessary in this kind of pattern is to "join on" the left to the right side, and the top to the bottom.

Progress in contemporary textile printing and weaving is very gratifying. Relation of materials to use, relation of design to its function (whether the design goes one way or all ways), choice of color, unusual textures, and skill in performance (Fig. 83) are the challenges which the textile designer-craftsman must meet.

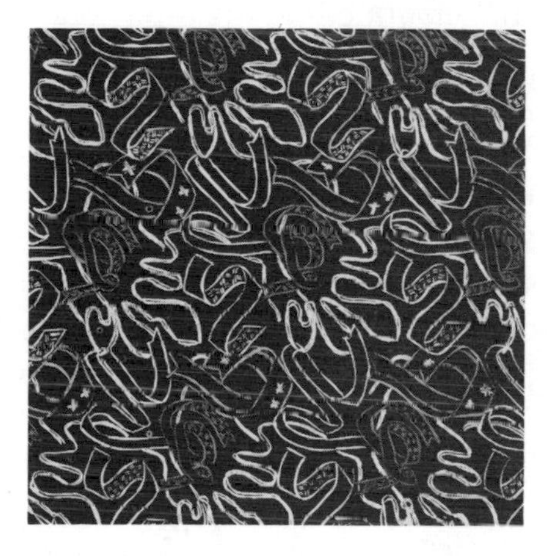

Fig. 84. The pattern must go "all ways" if it is a design for gift wrapping.

CHAPTER IV

DESIGN IN SKETCHING AND PAINTING

Drawing, value, color, texture

THE number of people who sketch and paint, whether for picture making or for designing, seems to be increasing in our time. Both the most respected head of our nation and the least respected citizen behind bars try their hand at it. Because there may be some who look upon sketching and painting as something unworthy of scientific investigation, yet who nevertheless are desirous of knowing more about what they do, let us consider a few simple principles which may be helpful.

Before we discuss these principles though, a word about how sketching is done would be appropriate. In the first place, a sketch is not a final drawing. There is a difference between a final drawing which has the freshness and spontaneity of a sketch (Fig. 85); and a sketch from nature used as a study for a final painting (Figs. 86, 87). Sketching is "feeling" on paper. Sketches are often working drawings *for* something. Figs. 88, 89. Many beginning students draw stiff decisive lines with a hard pencil on soft paper. This is the wrong way to do it. Use a soft pencil, preferably 4B to 6B, or a soft lithograph crayon which will ride easily over the paper. Employ your wrist, arm, mind, and feeling rather than your *fingers alone!*

Fig. 85. Marco DeMarco, "Head." This is a final drawing, although it skillfully incorporates the qualities of a spontaneous "sketch."

Fig. 86. Joseph McCullough. One of many sketches of a windmill.

Any one of the subjects mentioned in this chapter heading would require volumes of discussion for a full statement of their significance to the designer. Indeed there are hundreds of books written about drawing, and innumerable theories regarding the phenomenon of color—many of which are too belabored for the art student and probably even less appealing to the self-trained man in his home workshop.

Drawing, value, and color, in that order of importance, have a particular significance to us in the study of Basic Design.

Take, for example, the subject we have just studied—the design of a motif to be used for textiles. In drawing the motif, the parts which we *intend* to come forward must first be drawn in front of (Fig. 90) or "over" the other parts. Laws of perspective dictate that those in back are smaller than those in front, although in some modern paintings you may find artists reversing this principle, but let us be sure to draw one object in *"front of the other"* —whether the one in back is smaller or not. This enables the observer to understand what we mean. We have established which object recedes, and which object comes forward by "drawing" it that way. Drawing, then, is of primary importance.

Secondly, we must determine the value—the darkness or lightness—of each object as it is related to the particular value of background we choose. By this reasoning, color is less important than value. In other words, an object may be any color and still take its proper spatial position so long as it is (1) drawn correctly, and (2) has the right value in relation to the other values in the design.

Texture is last in this sequence of importance. It is an arbitrary

Fig. 87. Joseph McCullough, "Windmill." The final painting is the result of a discriminating selection from preliminary sketches.

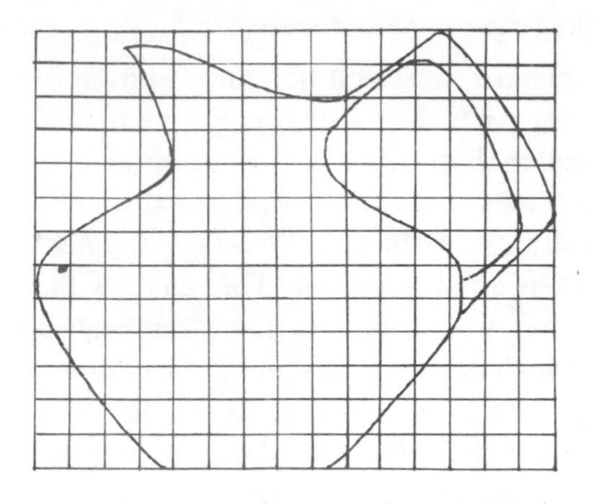

Figs. 88, 89. Frederick Miller, "Silver Water Pitcher." Sketches "for something" are often carefully planned drawings.

feature, to be employed by the designer or not as he chooses, as we shall see, beginning on page 102.

The word "drawing" has many meanings. The dictionary says that to draw is "to delineate, sketch, or portray." The arrangement of pieces of bent metal, tacks, or chunks of glass, is a form of drawing in the broader sense. This constitutes drawing because it delineates or portrays an emotion or idea. Drawing does not always imply a controlled line interpretation, or an outlined conception. Drawing for the designer means an expressive sketch in any medium which, for him, sufficiently conveys his idea. Finishing the design must not be overlooked by the designer either. Clumsy and ill-conceived shapes, lines, and spots can never be remedied by skillful handling of tools. The basic relationships, the organization, rhythms, and unity must be well conceived. The designer then proceeds to render with skill and conviction. Fig. 91. He may later refine edges, shapes, and passages of color.

Knowledge of structure is essential for the designer. How can a designer draw an imaginative leaf, fish, or bird, if he has not first grasped its actual structure? In the case of the leaf which grows from a stem, the designer feels that "upside down," "right for left," "large or small" are his personal liberties. But the art of utilizing these liberties becomes more genuine when he is experimenting with known facts rather than unknown facts. This, in a sense, makes drawing a prerequisite for designing.

No phase of art study can have greater importance than that of values (variations in tones from black to white). Everything in art is concerned with values. A large part of our existence—newspaper and other photographic documentation, movies, and television—is, in effect, communicated to us because our eyes interpret the meaning of dark and light. For example let us take our motif (Fig. 90), which is comprised of superimposed objects, lines, and shapes. We want this conception of superimposition to be *understood,* but unless we follow certain simple, academic rules, the objects which are placed in front may give the impression of being part of the background. They will appear more as a "hole" in the motif than as its foremost part.

We can best study this problem by considering how different value situations are handled by the designer in order to make his sketch or painting perfectly clear to the observer. To simplify our study of values let us speak of light (something white or lighter than middle value); middle (a value about half as dark as black and half as light as white); and dark (black, or a value darker than middle). With these three values we will set up three situations—one situation has a light background; one a middle background; and one a dark background. In the first situation (the light background), let us solve the problem of overlapping areas as simply as possible. We will utilize one set of values for the background, one for the middle distance, and one set of

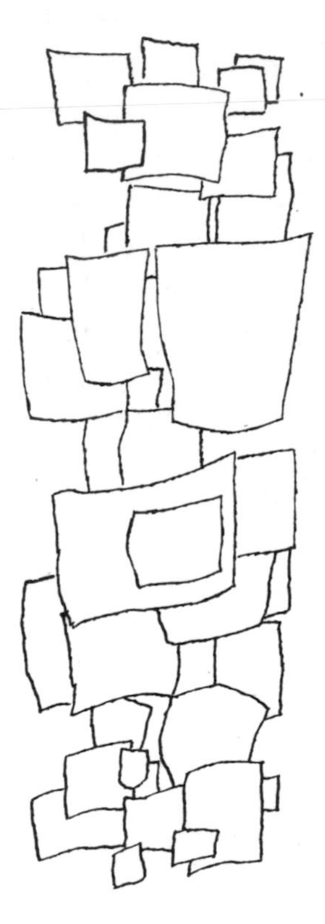

Fig. 90. When objects are meant to exist in more than one plane, one object must be drawn so as to appear in front of another.

values for the foreground objects. Our solution, in this situation, would be—background—light; middle distance—middle value; and foreground—darkest. So, in this case, as the objects seem to go back into the picture and are overlapped by the other objects,

Fig. 91. Paul Travis, "Tiger and Bull." Conviction, sureness of hand, and intuitive guidance contribute to this powerful message.

Fig. 92. The first value situation. Extreme distance is dead white. The observer represents theoretical black. Fig. 93. The second value situation—each object is lighter than the one behind it.

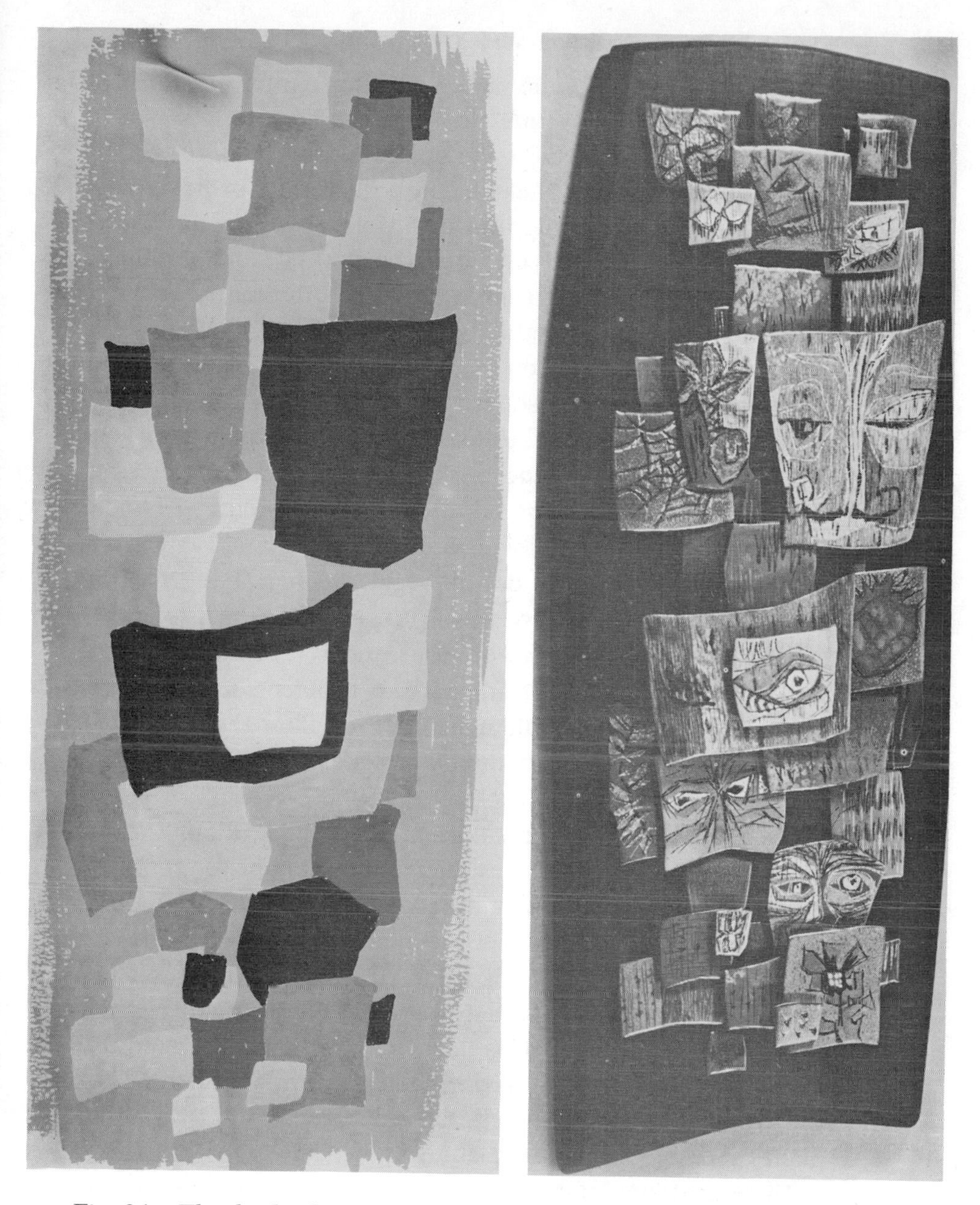

Fig. 94. The third value scheme. Objects are both lighter and darker than the background. Fig. 95. Kenneth F. Bates, "Still Life with Bosa", enamel panel. An example of "light on dark."

they become more like the background or lighter in value, Fig. 92. As we look at the picture we may imagine ourselves as being the source of darkness, and as an object approaches us it becomes darker, until it reaches the extreme foreground, or dead black. The effect is that of being in a dark forest looking out toward the light. The nearest trees would be darkest, and the middle distant trees lighter. The source of light from the sun or the extreme distance would be the lightest value.

Now, consider a situation which is the exact opposite. Presuming that we are now the source of light, and that we "light up" each object as it approaches us, our extreme distance, or background would now be the dark or theoretically, dead black. Objects which occur in the middle distance would be in middle values, and our foremost objects, lightest or white, Fig. 93. This simple scheme of values occurs regularly in still life painting, portraits, and the decorative arts. It is spoken of by artists as "light on dark" and is a safe, but obvious, method of making shapes take their rightful position in space. If problems in design were this easily solved one would need only to follow the above rules, but this becomes too confining. A designer may not always wish to present his ideas on a black background.

Let us think of a third situation, one which, though a little more involved, gives the designer much greater scope. In this instance we will chose the middle value as the background. The middle distance, or the parts of the motif which appear to be overlapped by the front parts, is now *either* darker *or* lighter than the background. So, also, the foreground pieces might be sometimes lighter and sometimes darker than the background, Fig. 94. This type of value situation will result in confusion unless the original drawing is a well-defined statement of overlapping planes and objects, and has what is known as "spatial existence."

There are times, of course, when we may go further and disregard all three of these theories, taking a completely arbitrary view but using the theories only when a plane or color refuses to stay in its intended position, Fig. 95.

THE MUNSELL COLOR THEORY

THREE CHARACTERISTICS OF COLOR

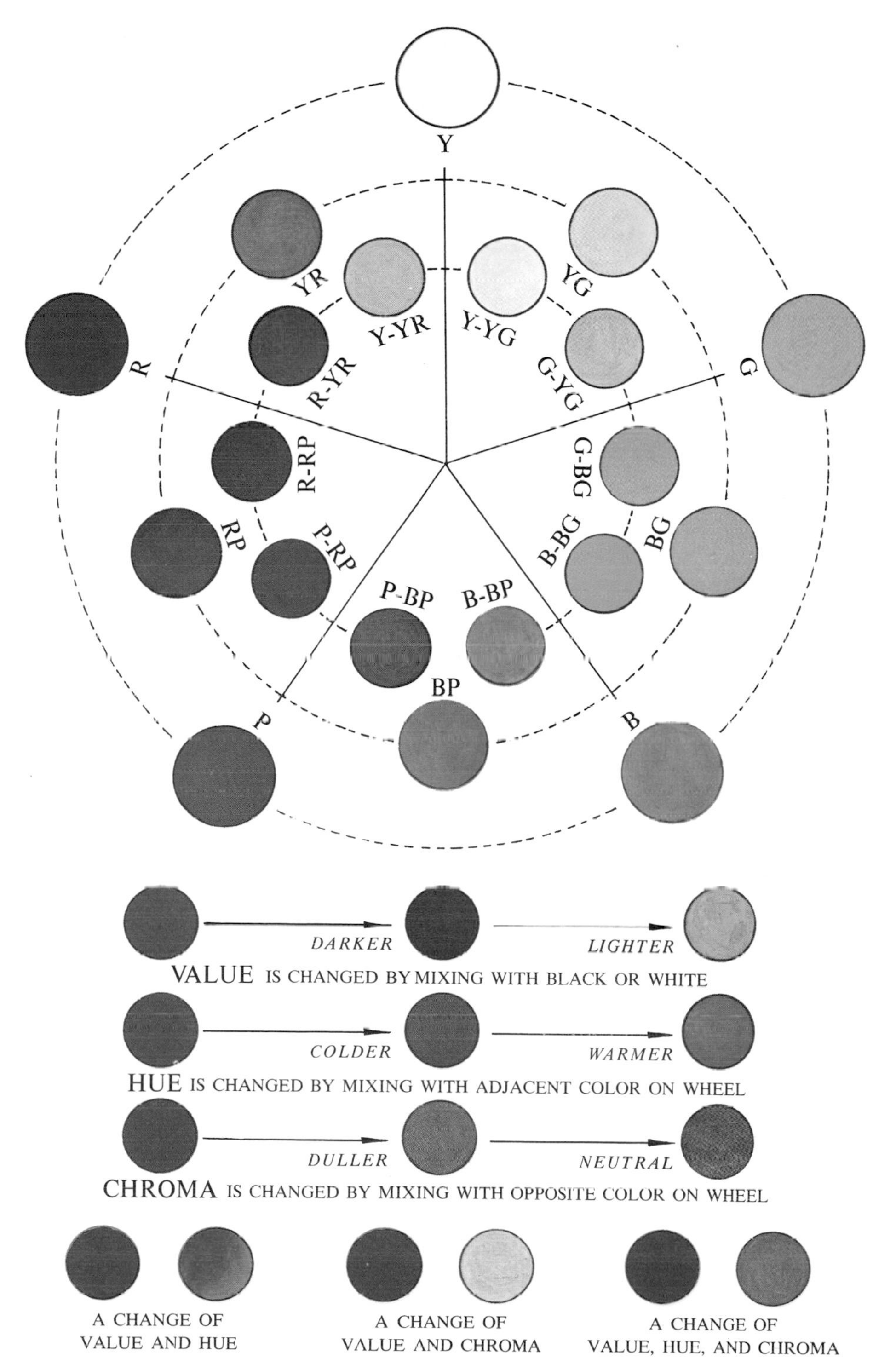

Though much has been said about the psychological effect of dark, light, or middle value colors, one can refute many of these dogmatic statements. It is said that "dark values are somber and morbid"—but what about the dramatic and exciting effect of a black-textured wall covering in a contemporary interior? Grays are supposed to be dull, pale, and uninteresting. This cannot be said of fine pottery which is dominantly grayish. We read that light values are weak, vapid, and effeminate. This is not always true. Strong lights and high values in paintings are often the means of expressing vitality, sharpness, and vigor.

Mood, or psychological effect upon the observer, is concerned with line, movement, spacing, juxtaposition, and rhythm as well as careful choice and arrangement of values. The contemporary artist, in fact, prefers to be liberated from the taboos about values. Pictures in middle values were much in vogue in the 1850's, but sombre scenes of cattle grazing in the meadows painted in middle or dark values have fortunately gone out of style. Students used to be warned against the use of black in paintings, but black used in paintings as bold outline or as large flat areas often predominates in an exhibition today. This was not the case in certain periods of our history. Changes in thinking and changes in style have brought about these releases. Taboos about how dark or light a sketch or painting should be are now a thing of the past.

Color is third in importance when it comes to making planes or objects exist in space. The object must first be drawn in front of another object if we intend it to take that position. Secondly, depending on the value of the background, the front objects must be in proper value relation to it. And thirdly, there is the color, which makes less difference to the object's position than the drawing and values do. An artist may want to paint a red apple in back *or* in front of a green apple. He cannot restrict his choice of apples to include only red apples in the foreground, and green apples in the background merely because he had learned a "rule" saying that red comes forward and green recedes! Our present dilemma, therefore, concerns a more detailed explanation of the meaning of "color." If red can be placed in back of green as well as before it and still hold its position, there must be certain *kinds* of reds that will behave where other kinds will not. What are these color characteristics, and how is the eye *accustomed* to accepting them?

Some of the early books on color theory strike us as being too pedantic. Social and economic conditions have played a part in changing our color tastes. Colors found in interiors, clothing, paintings, and art objects assume new phases with the change in fashions. Reaction to color is each person's prerogative. The layman who "knows nothing about art but knows exactly what he likes" often insists that his color taste is impeccable. It is the artist who knows what he wants but who also accepts the vastness of the subject of color. Some house-painters know by their "eye" or by their "sense" of color what to put into a pot of paint to make it more cheerful or subdued and this "feeling" for color is often more valuable than any theory. However, there is a workable theory for the designer—that which was evolved by Albert Munsell—and we shall consider it briefly.

Munsell uses eleven neutral value steps including black and white which theoretically are not colors but have a relation to color. This brings value five at the halfway point. Pure white is lighter than any color and called value ten. Jet black is darker than any color and is placed at the bottom of the scale as value zero. One should be able to detect a color value which is half as dark as black, and half as light as white, or value five. From this point the eye can be trained to detect a color value halfway between white and value five, and halfway between black and value five, and so on. Colors have certain levels in relation to the neutral value scale where they seem to be more normally recognized. For instance, yellow, as we know it, appears to be more like value nine (light) than purple. White must be added to purple to bring it *up* to value nine, and black added to yellow to *lower* it to value one. These distinctions refer to *color value* which theo-

Fig. 97. Persian Painting, 14th century. Persian paintings are superb examples of textural exploration and unified composition.

retically concerns only the darkness or lightness of the color. *Black in yellow does not make it duller, but only makes it darker.*

According to this theory, in order to make a color duller something else besides black must be added to it. This "dullness" characteristic of color is called "color chroma" and the neutralizing or dulling agent is *not* black or white. It is a color which is visually opposed to the original color. By arranging colors as they are seen in the rainbow around a circle we find that they appear to be well balanced. In so arranging the colors around the color wheel, the coldest are opposite the warmest. The color which is located exactly opposite on the color wheel appears more "unlike" that color than any other. This color, or "complement" to the other color, gives rise to an interesting phenomenon, for the admixture of these two in equal parts produces a completely neutralized effect, or gray. This phenomenon holds true with each set of complements and the mixture of complements is our only technical means of "dulling" or "subduing" a color.

Munsell proposes one other characteristic of color, that evolved when one color is mixed with the neighboring color on the wheel. This is a change of "hue," or a change in the coldness or warmth of a color. This change would also require a change of name. For example, a bluish kind of blue-green called "blue-blue-green" is warmer than a greenish kind of blue-green called "green-blue-green."

This much general information is required of any designer if he is to compound the colors he visualizes. Further information may not even be necessary. The value of a knowledge of *kinds* of color schemes such as complementary, triadic, split complements, double complements, set palettes, and so on, is doubtful. To say that complementary colors "go together" is as facetious as to state that they do not. When opposite colors are juxtaposed they seem to enhance each other, but the artist must still choose which value, chroma, and hue of these two colors to put side by side.

There is also the problem of proportion, "how much" of each to use. It is interesting to consider how the eye *customarily* accepts color in our everyday experiences. The eye is accustomed to observing the green of grass as warm and bright at close range, but the same kind of grass on distant hills appears as grayer and colder green. We conclude, then, that the more accustomed way of seeing color is "bright in front of dull," and "warm in front of cold." Secondly, because the landscape often contains larger amounts of dull green and smaller areas of bright colors the eye is accustomed to accept the following: "larger areas duller, smaller areas brightest." In sketching and painting these are not bad rules to follow, although it should not be taken too dogmatically. The designer should expect to strive for the *unaccustomed* as well as the *accustomed* in art. Color, of all the phases of design, cannot be controlled by a set of rules and at times it may be better to break them. An instructor cannot "give" a student a

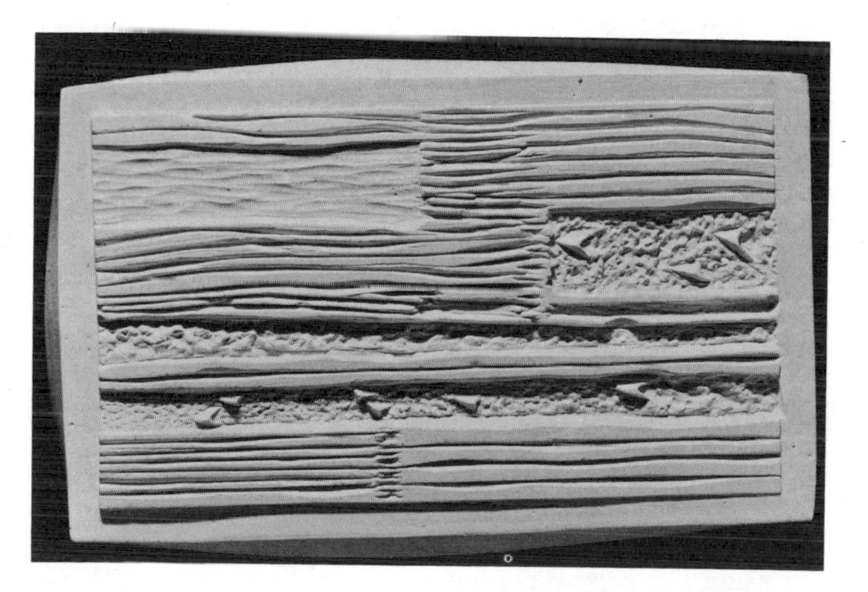

Fig. 98. A texture study resulting from gouging and carving plaster.

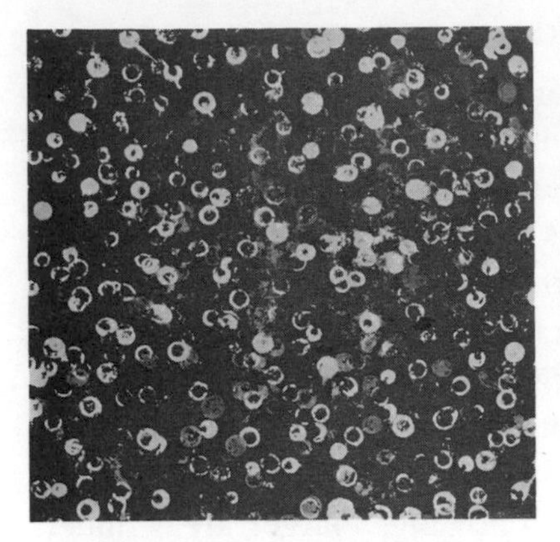

Fig. 99. Simple printing with a match stick or brush handle can produce an interesting textured surface.

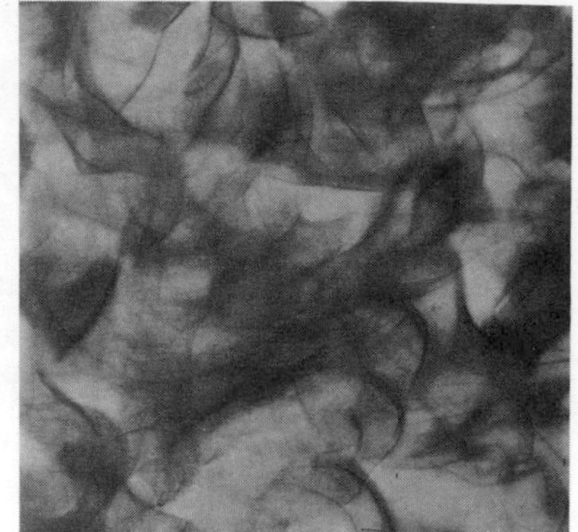

Fig. 100. Carbon from the smoke of a candle held near the paper created this kind of texture.

color sense, he can only discuss what the student has felt in regard to color and compare his reactions to those of the student.

The study of texture has a special design meaning for those who sketch and paint. No more superb illustration of "textural painting" can be found than in Persian painting of the fourteenth century, Fig. 97. The concern for textures in our painting today may in some way relate to economic unrest, or to our increased individual freedom. Smoothly shaded areas surrounded by hard stiff outlines give a conventional effect which reflects "decorative work" done in past decades. Free, broken, and textured outlines and surfaces embody a quality of freshness and add a more contemporary character to the work. The surfaces of objects or areas express a variety of "personalities" by their textures. Applying textures by a tool, a medium, or a technique takes on particular emphasis in contemporary designs. We can separate surface treatment into two categories—that of "directional" texture, and what might be called "static" texture. In the first case the strokes, either parallel or opposite to the dominant dimension, move the eye on the surface of that shape to enhance its direction. Brush strokes, gouges, streaks, and scratches serve

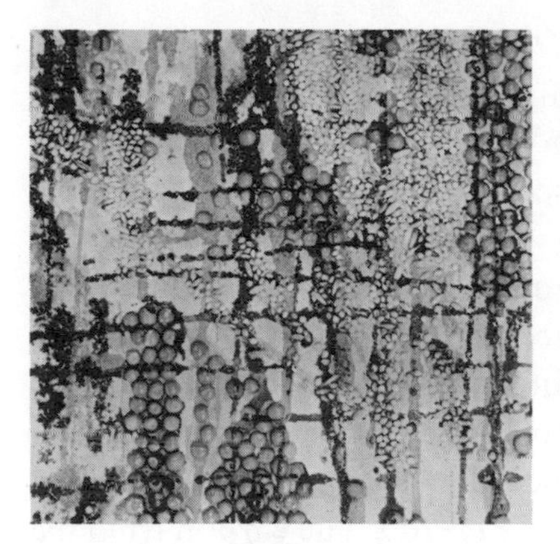

Fig. 101. Split peas and bird seed were utilized by this art student to gain unusual texture.

Fig. 102. This is a monoprint made by applying printer's ink to glass and printing with it (see text).

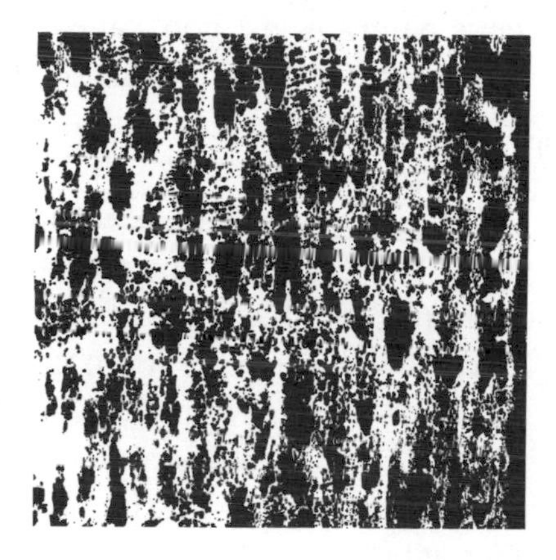

Fig. 103. The rubber cement resist method produces a texture unlike that of any other method (see text).

this purpose. Directional strokes may be applied "allover" as a pattern, or arbitrarily placed here and there.

Spotting, dotting, punching, and dabbing the surface gives another meaning to texture. This kind of textured surface is meant to enrich the area. Fig. 98. Texture as a result of a technique or tool has more intrinsic value than that which is superficially applied. Often both types are needed for enrichment. There is also texture which exists in the material itself such as wood grains, rough surfaces of paper, or canvas. Research from nature will aid us rather than discourage us. An assignment to invent new textures gives each individual an opportunity to make some purely aesthetic discoveries. For example, a simple process of printing, or stamping with a match stick, or the end of the brush handle which has been cut off and dipped in interesting tempera colors will produce an unusual effect (Fig. 99). In this case observe that the lighter spots come forward and the darker colored spots recede "into" the black background. A fascinating textural effect can also be achieved by allowing a lighted candle to be held under the paper. Fig. 100. The carbon from the flame is deposited in an unusual smokelike pattern. In a third instance, a colored tempera pattern was first applied, then glue or rubber cement in certain areas was used to hold split peas and bird seeds, Fig. 101. These in turn received various coats of tempera paint. A method called monoprinting will also produce unusual results. On a piece of glass, Duco cement is dribbled in an interesting pattern and allowed to dry. On another piece of glass apply printer's ink or oil paint and roll the brayer (linoleum block print roller) in it. Now proceed to print, using the first glass in the same way one prints with the linoleum block. The result is a free, organic kind of texture which is often suggestive of microscopic studies. Fig. 102. A final suggestion involves the application of a fairly heavy coat of rubber cement over colored paper or on a boldly painted tempera pattern. When this dries, rub certain areas with the finger and then cover the entire surface with India ink. After the ink dries remove the rubber cement which, of course, allows the ink to remain only in the places where the paper was exposed. Fig. 103. Sometimes an unusual texture is obtained by allowing the rubber cement, which is coated with the ink, to peel away, leaving a weblike effect. These experiments and ones which you will invent for yourself are fascinating. In these areas, where the student is released from the difficulties of drawing and design theories, his results are bound to be a true expression of personal taste and creativity.

CHAPTER V

DESIGN IN SCULPTURE, CERAMICS, AND POTTERY *Realism, stylization, superimposed decoration*

THE preceding chapters have covered some of the ground work in the study of Basic Design. But there are also more individualistic aspects to our work and among the first we might consider are realism, Fig. 104, and stylization, Fig. 105.

In sculpture or ceramic sculpture, as in any art expression, one needs to understand the "style" or manner in which each person prefers to work. And furthermore, that style must be consistently manifested in all parts of the design.

We are confronted with the problem of designing in three dimensions. Whether two-dimensional study (drawing, painting, graphics, etc.) should precede three-dimensional study (modeling, jewelry, crafts, etc.) is not a point which needs to be proved—a knowledge of design is essential to both. When one approaches a chunk of clay for the first time the tactile quality—the physical act of handling it—must be considered. So often a proficient student of design fails to apply his knowledge to a problem in a three-dimensional medium; it is possible, in fact, that some artists who do not conceive form may yet be excellent draftsmen and colorists.

Figs. 104, 105. Compare the "stylization" of trees below with the illustration on the left, both by the same artist. Some of the facts are here, but some, such as branches, bark, and foliage, are left out.

Our main concern now is with applying the same sense of organization, rhythm, and balance, which we have discussed, to a three-dimensional object, Fig. 106. We are not to look, think, or feel only from the front of the piece we are modeling, for it has many sides. What were called negative *areas* are now negative *volumes,* which must be designed and related just as carefully as the positive masses of the clay itself, Fig. 107. From the first conception, which includes the construction of armatures for strength, we must learn to observe and *feel* what is happening from the top, bottom, sides, and front.

Keep in mind that in designing for sculpture you must first visualize the whole idea of what you want to achieve; secondly, that the forms must have a feeling of belonging together, which includes your concern for the negative spaces; thirdly, that your style or "way" of designing must be consistent in all parts; and lastly—and of great importance—is the fact that you must realize that you are working with light and dark (a deep incision casts a darker shadow than a shallow one, and an abrupt bend

Fig. 106. Peter Voulkos, salt glaze stoneware. A superb example of an inherent sense of form, balance, and integrated decoration.

Fig. 107. Henry Moore, "Reclining Figure." Masterful handling of negative and positive masses is seen in this famous sculptor's work.

in the surface makes a sharper shadow edge than a soft bend, Fig. 108).

Let us begin our "ways of thinking" about creating a three-dimensional object—the essence of sculpture—with "realism," Fig. 109.

REALISM

What place does realism have in our study of Basic Design? First, we need to have a clear understanding of the meaning of the word, and particularly that it denotes something different from "naturalism." A naturalistic portrayal of an object is a literal translation of it as it appears in nature. Naturalistic interpretation, in fact, approximates photography, and is useful for scientific drawings, botanical and medical research plates.

Realism, surrealism, superrealism, and magic realism are art terms, all of which have to do with reality rather than idealization. In each case the term implies more than "naturalism." It implies some exaggeration. Realism forces the drawing and heightens the colors as observed in nature, Fig. 110; surrealism

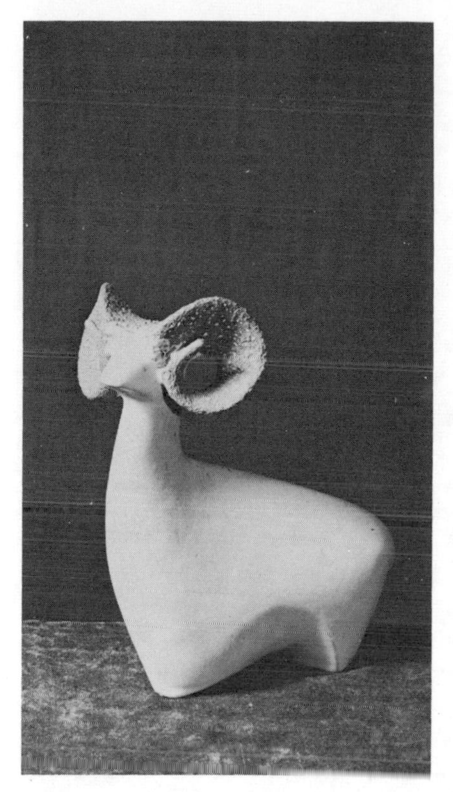

Fig. 108. Charles Lakofsky, "Horned Animal." Notice the difference in shadows made by "soft" bends of the surface, and abrupt or "sharp" bends. The deeper you penetrate the form, the stronger the shadow.

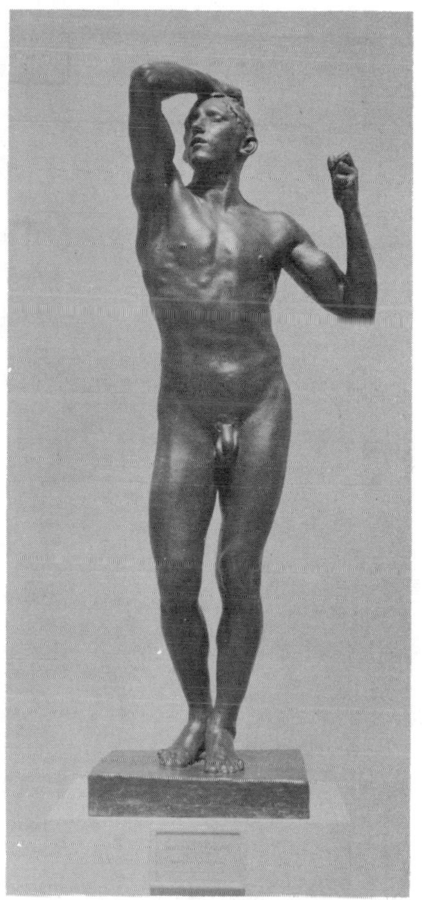

Fig. 109. Auguste Rodin, "Man of the Age of Bronze." Rodin was accused of making a mold from life in this supreme example of three-dimensional realism.

Fig. 110. John James Audubon, "The Great White Heron." This print might be described as "forced naturalism," or realism.

Fig. 111. Henri Julien Rousseau, "The Jungle, Tiger Attacking a Buffalo" (detail). This might be labeled "Superrealism." Each design element is forced by the arbitrary use of the light source.

treats reality irrationally, Fig. 112; superrealism overexaggerates nature, Fig. 111; and magic realism deals with imaginative facts and situations but portrays them in a literal way, Fig. 113. In each of these classifications, however, there is one element in common which differentiates them from naturalism. That element is the designer's privilege of composing the objects as he pleases. Composing, arranging, or "designing" is not an essential part of naturalistic interpretation.

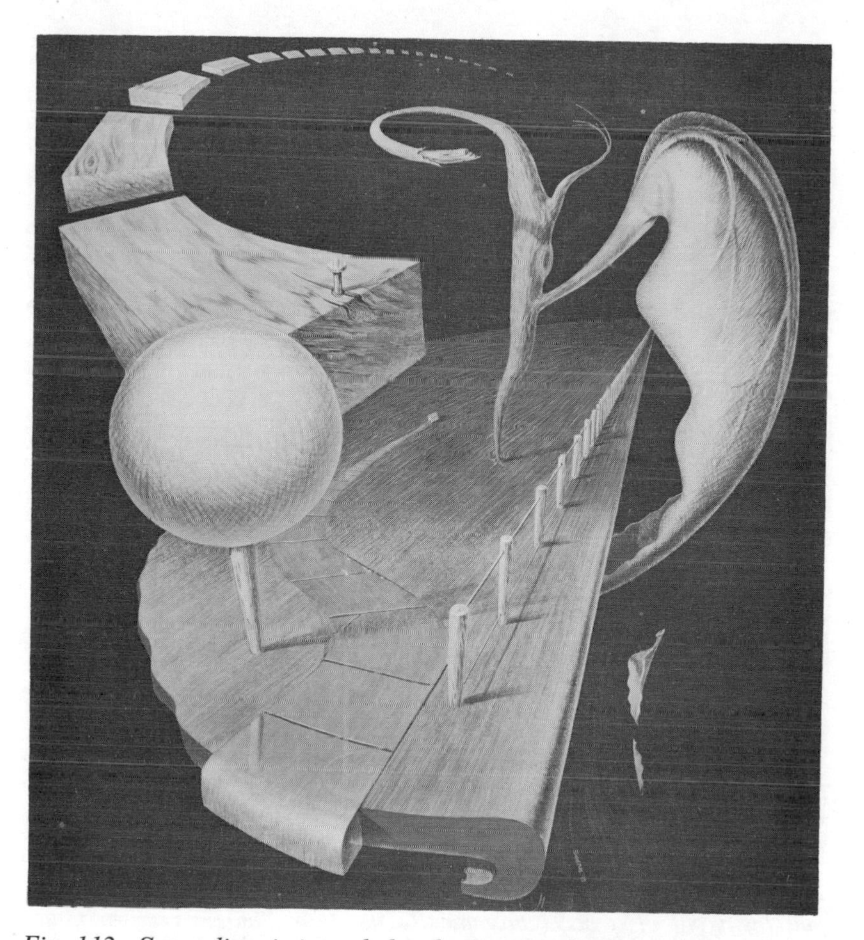

Fig. 112. Surrealism is intended to be irrational. These objects do not exist except in the mind of the artist when he dreams.

Fig. 113. Paul Riba, "The Bells." Objects, much as a magician might pull them out of a hat (consequently the term "magic realism"), are portrayed with exquisite detail, as in reality.

Realistic studies are of unquestionable value to the designer. Observation of natural phenomena builds up his repertoire of known facts. His vocabulary of textures, shapes, rhythms, and colors becomes a springboard for his imagination. In order to make a design interpretation "of a thing," one should become absorbed in knowing more about it, at least more than a casual observation of it reveals. Often in modeling the object realistically one makes certain succinct discoveries. One discovers that objects as they exist are not outlined; that a tree, for instance, is visible to the eye only because it has a different value or color from the one next to it, or from the background against which it is seen. Outlines are merely a device of the artist who wishes to portray three-dimensional objects on a two-dimensional piece of paper.

The knowledge of texture and structure, in fact, is increased through realistic studies. How does a leaf grow from a stem; what direction do the hairs grow on this or that animal; what is the anatomical structure of a feather? The answers should be found before proceeding with other styles. Conscientious realistic

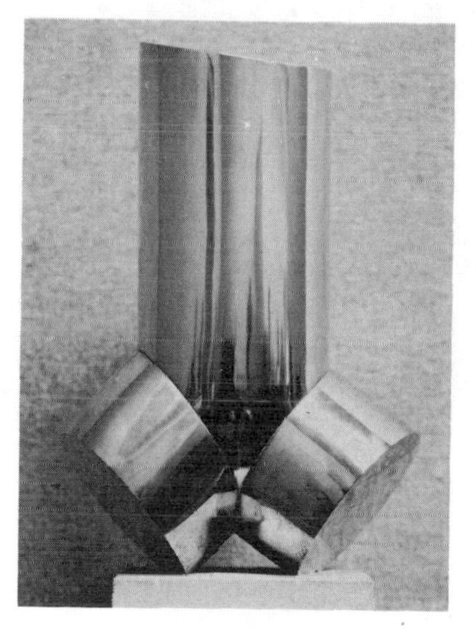

Fig. 114. Constantin Brancusi, "Torso." Brancusi has resorted to extreme stylization in rendering the human body as polished brass cylinders.

studies are of lasting benefit as evidenced in much of our contemporary sculpture. A powerful realistic statement may have more art value than a dull abstract understatement. Nature presents, on *occasions,* certain forms, growths, and textures which more or less warrant the artist's acceptance of them in a realistic manner.

STYLIZATION

The term "stylization" covers a wide field of techniques and mannerisms, Fig. 114. Dr. Thomas Munro, in his book *The Arts and Their Interrelations,* The Liberal Arts Press, 1949, New York, has given the subject of "style" a thorough and complete explanation. In part he says: "Recent developments in art history have

Fig. 115. The ways of varying the stylization of a leaf are infinite.

laid great stress on styles and style trends running all through the arts of a certain period. Vast as they are, such trends in artistic style are never independent, but parts of still larger cultural trends embracing all forms of thought and behaviour, social, political, economic, religious and scientific. . . . There is no cultural trend . . . apart from human individuals. . . . We see the artist as never entirely original, never a bolt from the blue, always responsive to the currents about him, and therefore different from what he would have become in another cultural setting. . . . In every period, certain basic conceptions and techniques are taken for granted by the vast majority of artists. A general style . . . never exactly determines the individual styles of its adherents. It moves them toward a general orientation of seeing, thinking, feeling and imagining."

To stylize a subject the sculptor should have some knowledge of that subject. Having studied the bird, animal, tree, or figure, let us say that we intend to change its proportions, simplify its contours and eliminate details, but that we do not disregard the original structure. This, in effect, is what we mean by making a "stylized" leaf design from a leaf, Fig. 115. It is "one step" away from nature. As we progress with other styles we will take further liberties with nature.

For a specific example consider a stylized head, Fig. 116. The shape may be extended in any way, more pointed, Fig. 117; thinner, fatter, with a change of proportion, Fig. 118; or features exaggerated. These changes have not altered the fact that the head is a mass with certain accepted features such as nose, mouth, and eyes. Each artist arrives at his own interpretation, but we still recognize a head as a head, not something else, Fig. 119.

No two sculptors would "stylize" in the same way. The sculptures of William McVey (Fig. 120) do not look like those of Carl Milles (Fig. 121), but both sculptors' work could be classified as "stylistic."

As the design student increases his observation of shapes,

Figs. 116, 117, 118, 119. A sketch of the head suggests stylistic interpretation to the sculptor. Lines, proportions, and features become elon-

forms, and colors in nature he is aware of the fact that certain ones exist *as* stylizations. For example, the hawk (Fig. 122), so magnificently stylized in Egyptian sculpture, is already stylistic to some extent in nature.

The words "stylized" and "decorated" are often confused. "Stylized" refers to design according to a particular individualistic point of view. "Decorated" implies a "decoration" superimposed upon something and although the word is sometimes used in bad faith, it describes a device which professional artists often use superbly, Fig. 123. Historically many examples exist of superimposed decoration which nicely prove that it is possible to enrich the surface without detracting from the basic idea. On the other hand, we are constantly confronted with objects which are in poor taste because they are poorly "decorated," or embellished. Some stores are burdened with everyday articles unnecessarily embellished. It would appear that too often a manufacturer feels that in order for an article to sell, it must have decoration *applied to it.* But simple sculptures need little "decoration." Their beauty is in their stylistic form as conceived by a mature artist. Fig. 120.

gated and simplified. Amedeo Modigliani's "Head" incorporates all of the theories we have discussed concerning stylization.

Before we leave the subject of stylization let us list the designer's intentions as he makes a stylized object for sculpture or ceramics: these are: *simplification* of form, technique, details, anatomy, and naturalistic information (Fig. 114); *exaggeration* of certain characteristics (Fig. 175); *dramatization* of scale, lighting, and proportion (Fig. 108); and *consistency* of individualistic mannerisms throughout. An object, of course, can be slightly stylized or highly stylized.

The decoration of pottery raises certain problems of its own. In "Aesthetics and the Artist" by Thomas Munro, published in the *Journal of Aesthetics and Art Criticism,* XI:8 (June, 1953), he says, "It is part of the contemporary artist's metier to learn how to practice some of the chief styles of the past, so as to know better how to devise new ones of his own." This applies particularly to the problem of superimposing decoration on a given form such as pottery.

Many times a good pot is ruined by a wrong choice of decoration. Toshiko Takaezu shows extreme sensitivity in her choice of decoration for pots and bowls. Sometimes one skillfully planned or "deeply felt" brush stroke is her answer, Fig. 126. Decoration

Fig. 120. William McVey, "Introspective." Notice the extreme simplification of hands and feet, the intentional absence of anatomical detail in the chest, nose, feet, legs, and so on.

Fig. 121. Carl Milles, "Triton with Shells." Although Milles and McVey might both be labeled as "stylistic sculptors," each artist's work is clearly identifiable.

Fig. 122. Egyptian Sculpture, "Hawk-God, Horus," XXX Dynasty. Egyptian sculpture, with its monumental and majestic forms, has often been called the greatest sculpture ever created by man.

Fig. 123. Ann Chapman, "Horse" (contemporary). Superimposed decoration can be most effective. The panels of enrichment are structurally related to the horse's form.

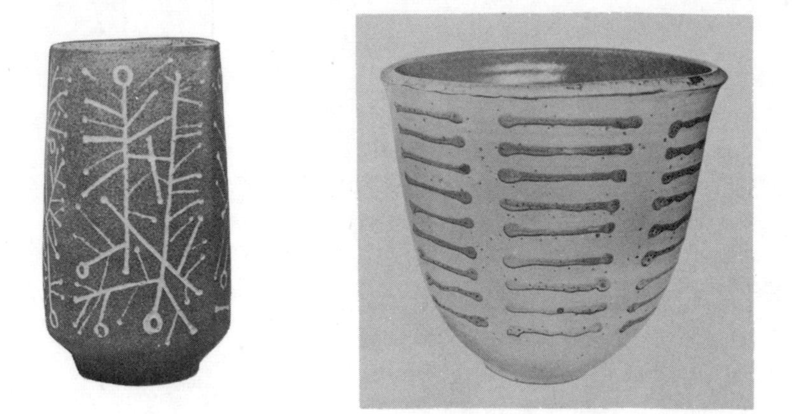

Fig. 124. Aaron Bohrod, designer; Carlton Ball, potter. Informal decoration. The motifs are not built on the structural lines of the pot. Fig. 125. Charles Mosgo. Formal decoration. Each part of the decoration is based on the structural lines of the pot.

in the form of incising, sgraffito, or textural glazes can be grouped under two headings; formal, relating to the structure lines of the pot (Fig. 125); and informal, not related to the structure lines (Fig. 124). But certainly the superimposed decoration must enhance the pot's form or not be there at all. Many potters feel that the character of the clay or the glazes used supply all the decoration that is needed. Refer to Chapter IV regarding the types of texture which can be studied. The artist's feeling for stylization can be appropriately utilized in a medium such as molded or etched glass. Let us make a positive statement then regarding realism, stylization, and superimposed decoration. In sculpture, or ceramic sculpture, there is a place for realism, if a portrayal of an event or situation warrants such a factual interpretation. But realism is far different from abject naturalism—or the copying of nature. It is the difference between a life mask cast and a fine bronze portrait. This is not to imply, however, that sculpture *should* be realistic.

In pottery rarely, if ever, would one find the excuse to use any form of realism or stylization. How often one sees vases and pots which are meant to be used as flower containers (sometimes in our better stores) with realistic or stylized flowers painted *on* them! The flowers should be in the pots, not on them. The pot without the flowers must be as beautiful as it is with the flowers. This is a fact that every good potter knows, but unfortunately, one which not every merchant or every customer recognizes.

Fig. 126. Toshiko Takaezu, stoneware pot. One or two "deeply felt" brush strokes complete this pot. A fascinating example of appropriate superimposed decoration.

CHAPTER VI

DESIGN IN MOSAICS, ENAMELS, AND JEWELRY

Conventional, geometric, and abstract styles

THE making of mosaics, enamels, and jewelry has increased in popularity in the last decade, but the fact that more people are trying their hand at these crafts does not guarantee increased proficiency in design. China painting, as a craft, became more or less extinct in the first decade of this century because good design was not always considered along with the enthusiasm for doing it. Some of our crafts suffer in the same way, and knowledge of the principles of basic design was never more needed than today. Let us consider the particular problems of designing in each of these crafts separately and then return to the styles mentioned above.

MOSAICS

Our first thought in planning a design for mosaics is pattern. The success of the mosaic design depends largely on the skillful placing of flat areas one against the other, Fig. 127. The function of a mosaic must be taken into consideration. It is primarily a mural decoration, the word "mural" being derived from the French word "mur" (wall). Our reasoning should be simple. It is to enhance, or enrich the surface of the wall. Therefore, almost without exception, our design should not stress the illusion of great depth and space. Let us accept this premise and minimize the exceptions.

We no longer have to think in three dimensions, but there is one feature which we must not overlook. That is the distance between the mosaic and the viewer. The mosaic is not an object to be held in the hand, or even one which will be viewed from arm's length. This design must "carry." The pattern we create must be strong enough, or in some cases, subtle enough, to warrant distant viewing. The original color sketch should be made in its actual scale, placed on the wall, and viewed in the normal way. I find this to be one of the most neglected practices of art students. The allover effect, the drawing, pattern, and perspective, is distorted when the design is seen horizontally on the desk.

In addition to pattern, color, and texture are two major concerns in designing a mural. What style an artist adopts to design the mural is purely personal and in this chapter we will include

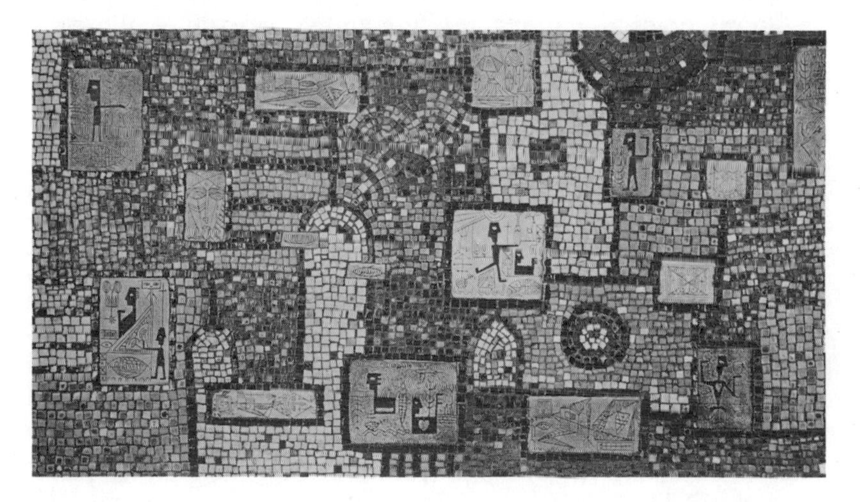

Fig. 127. David Holleman, wall mosaic. A two-dimensional design depends largely on the skillful arrangement of flat areas, an essential factor in mosaic designs.

three more categories of style: conventional, geometric, and abstract.

Texture is obtained by the characteristics of the medium itself. This is one of its greatest charms. No two tesserae are exactly alike in color, shape, or size. But one must guard against too much texture which can approximate a "speckled" look. Preliminary texture studies in plaster are helpful to the student, Fig. 98. By contrasting certain parts of solid colors, either as lines, spots, or areas, with more strongly textured surfaces, one is able to control the emphasis and meaning of the entire composition. The craft of mosaics, like enameling, can be extremely disappointing if the designer overlooks the importance of color. Too often one sees mosaics in literal colors (blue sky, green leaves, and an attempt to make realistic figures), but because of the peculiar qualities involved in building the pattern from tiny pieces, it may well be a mistake to attempt a realistic effect in mosaics. The most famous examples of mosaics are Byzantine, which are seldom realistic, but highly decorative and stylized. Because the contemporary tile mosaics are more abstract, they are, in my opinion, more fascinating and successful as an expression of the medium.

ENAMELS

Enameling on metal is one of our most popular crafts today. Enameling, like no other medium, *seems* to be "easy to do" but there are many pitfalls for the amateur. The brilliance and sparkle achieved by quick firing is only one factor which is responsible for its attractiveness. Thorough knowledge of design principles is more essential and should supersede technical "know-how."

Let us consider a few hints for designing an enamel piece. Take the problem of the design for a simple round tray. There is no reason to deny that a circle *is* a circle. The problem is to find a design suited to a circle rather than some other shape. Again,

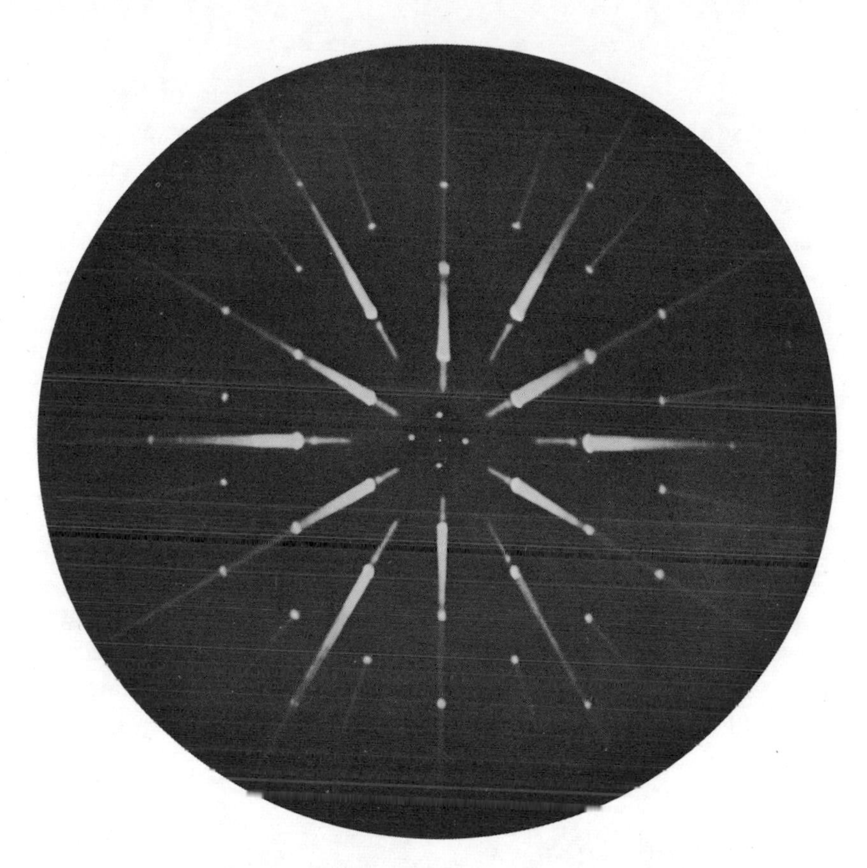

Fig. 128. A rare X-ray photograph of a single ice crystal. By universally accepted standards this is a good design, and one of the many natural phenomena which remain a mystery to man.

we stress simplicity. Great designs have been created for the circle. Illustrated is an X-ray photograph of a single ice crystal, Fig. 128. This design has universal appeal. Study it carefully. It is simple, but not *obvious.* There are many intriguing relationships and subtleties which raise the design from the commonplace to the unusual. These are also relationships to strive for when designing a simple, formally balanced, round enameled tray.

For the informally balanced round tray even more restraint must be used. The design motif is to be thought of only as something which enhances, not destroys, the roundness of the circle, otherwise the function of the tray is forfeited. A tray, as such, is not the place for a pictorial illustration. Historically, enamels have been produced which were somewhat realistic, but they were not used as decorative ash trays!

Technically, an enamel must give the appearance of being embedded "into" the surface, not painted "on" the surface. This principle might help us in designing. The motif should not be a motif of arbitrary size, but one which is scaled to have a sense of belonging to the size of the circle chosen.

In regard to free forms such as the long shape shown (Fig. 129), one might experiment by relating a motif "with the shape," "across the shape," or "all over the shape." In each case there must be a structural relationship to the shape chosen.

Enameling is a craft concerned with more than the making of trays. It embraces such forms as plaques, pictures, wall decorations, and murals. Study of theories concerning composition and space filling should be part of the enamelist's background and

Fig. 129. Kenneth F. Bates, "Pointes d'Or," enamel tray. One way to compose a free form is to place motifs in direct opposition to the shape.

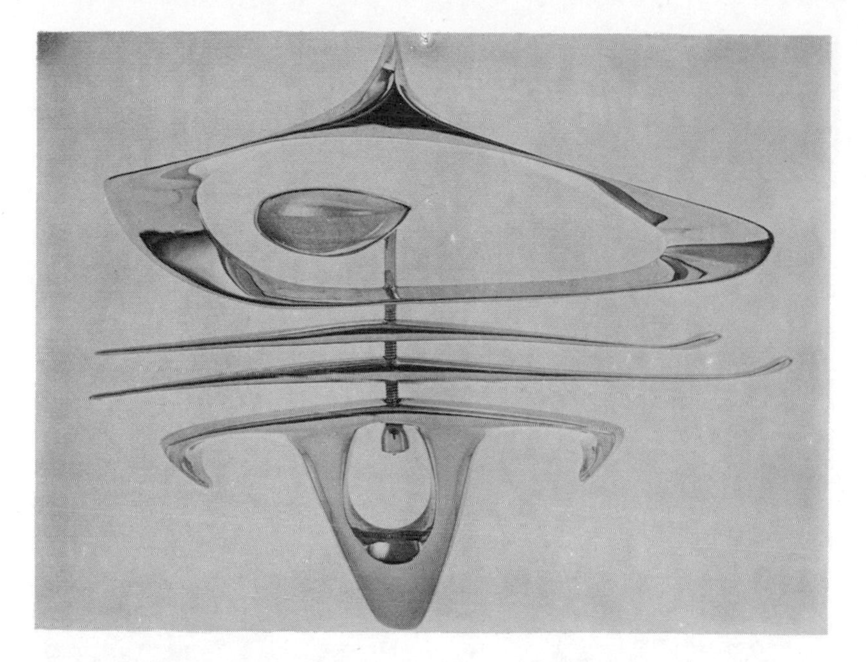

Fig. 130. Svetozar Radakovich. In this outstanding example of modern jewelry, Svetozar Radakovich has forged *many of the parts such as the horizontal bars and elliptical ring at the top.*

will be covered in subsequent chapters. Perhaps the finest use of enameling is its application to and its combination with jewelry.

JEWELRY

The practice of ignoring design principles when working with precious metals and glowing jewels is too prevalent with the hobbyist. He is entranced with the properties of the metal but not willing to explore them. Jewelry can become tawdry if over-embellished, and dull if void of any form of enrichment. Thin, flat metal gives the effect of being "tinny" whereas too heavy metal becomes bulky and awkward.

Contemporary jewelry makes abundant use of the filed, forged (Fig. 130), and cast three-dimensional forms. These processes constitute the difference between "bent" metal, and "formed"

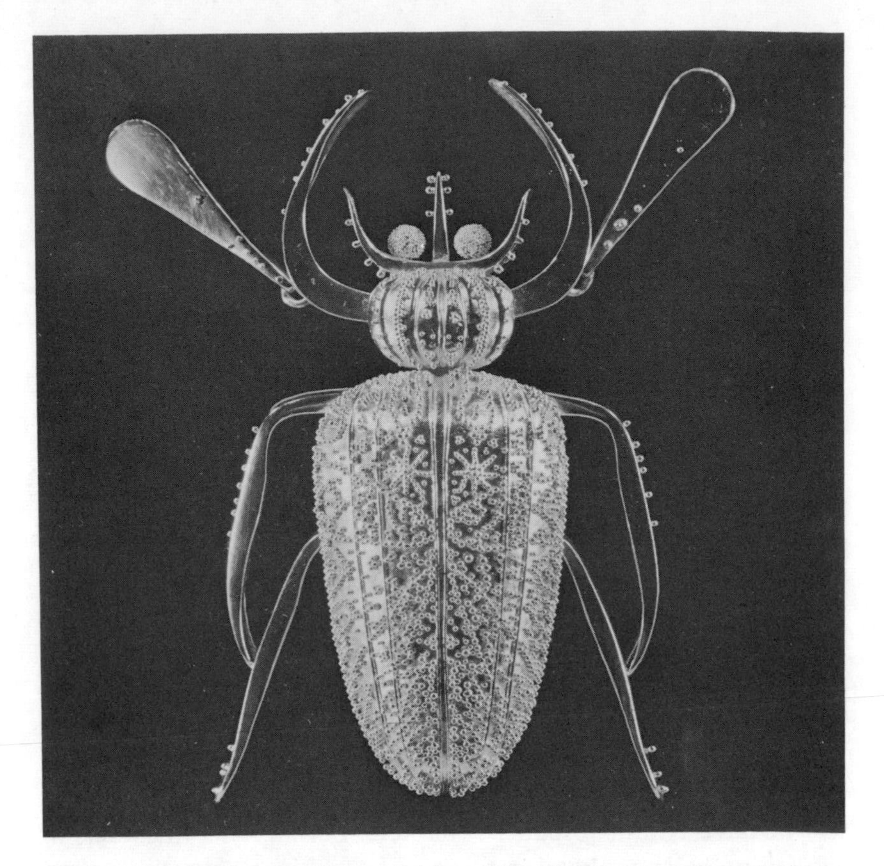

Fig. 131. John Paul Miller, necklace (detail). In this enlarged photograph of Mr. Miller's exquisite beetle you can see the surface enrichment called granulation, a complicated fusing process.

metal. In the beetle shown it will be noticed how well the highly enriched surface—granulation—(Fig. 131) can be contrasted with highly refined or smooth surfaces.

If possible, make the sketches of your ideas to scale. Professionally, the completely rendered sketch in full color is usually submitted to the client before the craftsman begins his work. This is a good idea for the nonprofessional also. The theories and principles of design presented in the first three chapters should be applied in the making of preparatory drawings.

Allowing himself to be enchanted by the glitter of polished metal and the sparkle of jewels at the sacrifice of good design is a common fault of the amateur when making his first piece of jewelry.

CONVENTIONAL STYLE

Further explanation is required about the terms "conventional," "geometric," and "abstract" if we are to have a wider

Fig. 132. Plaque, Panama, Coclé. This beaten gold plaque from an ancient culture has a quality of timelessness. It is a most ingenious example of the human figure used bisymmetrically.

knowledge of a particular *style* we wish to use when designing jewelry and other items.

Conventionalizing an object appears to take it further from nature than stylizing it. Here we are actually held down by a set, or formal type of balance, Fig. 132. Most of our discussion about contemporary design up to this point, in fact, has been concerned with the asymmetric balance, or balance of unequal parts. Avoid-

Fig. 133. Kenneth F. Bates, enameled spherical box. The knob or finial should relate to the whole design of the box. In this case a conventional motif, which divides the box into twenty-four equal parts, has a finial with eight parts.

ing stiff formality in rendering and conception has been our aim. However, as designers, we should not disregard work of past centuries where formal design was often very handsome. Numerous instances in nature thrill us with the precision and elegance of their formal or regular repetition. By formal balance we mean exact duplication of the motif or parts of it on the left and right, or repeated around a point. We can think of instances where formal repetition would be more appropriate than informal. Suppose the article in consideration is the finial or knob to a symmetrically shaped box, Fig. 133. Here, if the knob is also symmetrically formed, any decoration placed upon it would be in better taste if it were formal rather than informal. The form or shape of the knob is primary, the decoration secondary.

For a plate whose edge is subdivided or scalloped, some formal pattern or even repetition based on the structure of the plate (or number of scallops) would be in better taste than motifs scattered at random. Structure or structural lines of an object are of major importance to a designer-craftsman. Structural lines are the lines upon which the object is built. The structural lines of a square or circle are the diameters, diagonals, and concentric shapes within. In a free or asymmetric shape the same holds true. There would be the long and short axes, and the inner shapes whose sides are parallel to the contour. We might also combine both free and formal design. An informal motif might be placed within a structural area. Many instances in nature reveal this kind of "nonconventional within conventional" type of design. You will find this principle well demonstrated in the structure of a dragonfly's wings.

Whether we are speaking of symmetry or asymmetry, there is seldom "unbalance" in the life around us. Balance is that quality without which life would become unpleasant. When we look at the Leaning Tower of Pisa we do not feel right about it, we feel *uncomfortable.* In the presence of a person who is malformed our sympathy is aroused, and we wish that he were not "out-of-

Fig. 134. Calico, 17th century. Though not contemporary in character, this nevertheless represents skilled and sensitive work.

balance." But on the other hand, there can be a subtle balance of *uneven* parts, *felt* by the artist, which is not rationalized. The amoeba, for instance, a one-celled animal, is balanced in an asymmetric manner. To "feel" balance is to "feel" unbalance. Balance of the unexpected in design, "balance of the unbalance," concerns the artist at all times.

To return to our study of conventional design, it is important to remember that the term "conventional" is not quite synony-

Fig. 135. We might prefer the same design elements with a more contemporary interpretation.

mous with "formal." A person might dress and act informally, yet he would be called a conventional person if he repeated these acts day after day. A conventional person is disinterested in anything which does not conform to his established pattern and this description also applies to conventional design. Conventional style implies a repetition of the factors or elements of a design.

Truly conventional design may have less appeal for the con-

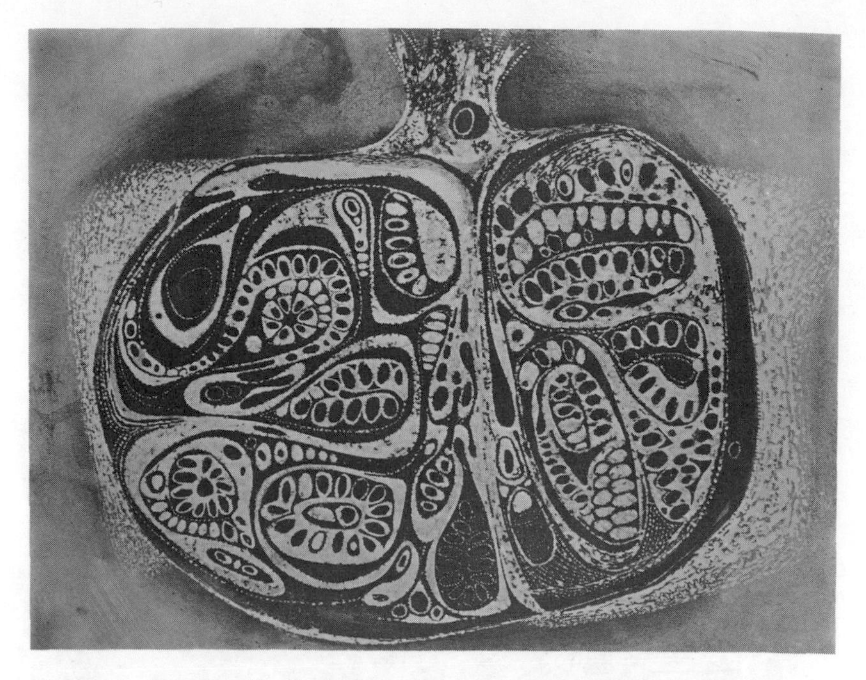

Fig. 136. Douglas H. Pickering, "Pomegranate." Outside shape, structure, seeds, and seed "pockets" have been used by the artist in this ink drawing, yet the result is purely contemporary.

Figs. 137, 138. A formal design composed of informal shapes for a circular tray can be reinterpreted as an informal design.

temporary artist than for certain primitive peoples. Scallops, frets, spirals, and tendrils are seldom employed today, at least not in a set conventional manner. Our scallops have become uneven, our frets asymmetric, and our spirals warped. Stiff double outlines have disappeared, the cautiously drawn line has become the rapid dry brush stroke, the trite "S" curve is more of a bent curve. *Neatness has less virtue than freshness in art!* These changes in style are related to changes in our way of life. *But the artist should avoid following the fashion of the day so closely that he himself becomes conventional in doing so.*

A conventional design, of course, is not necessarily a bad design but it may well be if handled sentimentally. A mosaic, enameled tray or silver earring could be contemporary in style even though designed conventionally. We do not feel like condemning oriental rugs, or fine brocade, and calico designs, which are conventional in style even though we may prefer them in a freer style, Figs. 134, 135. They represent the work of sensitive craftsmen. It is when we duplicate these designs without adapting them to our own way of life that we, as designers, become conventional. We can use the Persian pomegranate motif in a new way (Fig. 136), with new colors and new interpretation. No artist *possesses* the pomegranate, nor can he claim its obsolescence. The Egyptian lotus blossom and the French fleur-de-lis are conventional designs which belong to a given period, but any artist may interpret them as unconventional designs if he pleases. Try your hand at two interpretations of the same motif for a circular tray—one formal (Fig. 137), and one informal (Fig. 138).

GEOMETRIC STYLE

Natural forms and objects about us seldom have contours that are strictly mechanical. The compass and the straight edge are inventions of man. To create a design using only these two instruments is therefore a considerable deviation from nature. There

Fig. 139. This photograph has the appearance of a contemporary painting, but in actuality, it is a photograph of halite, rock salt.

Fig. 140. Lyonel Feininger, "The Steamer, Odin II." Feininger's painting represents an interesting parallelism with the rock salt crystals.

is, nevertheless, intriguingly complex geometric structure in many natural objects such as shells, pine cones, snakes, and rock crystals (Fig. 139). Observe how certain artists have made use of these phenomena in painting, Fig. 140.

Students of design are sometimes misled by the term "geometric." It is a serious misconception to think that a geometric interpretation of an object is nothing more than "straightening the edges with a ruler, and drawing the curves with a compass." Nothing could be further from the truth. Much more invention and ingenuity than that is required on the part of the artist to make a good geometric design. Perhaps less drawing ability is required but *not* less imagination.

By the geometric attitude in design we imply a certain kind of simplification of basic shapes and lines which impose a still greater restriction than mere stylization. To create your design in the geometric manner for craftwork, start by thinking *with* the instruments. Lines, circles, squares, oblongs, triangles, and quadrants may be manipulated until some pleasing combination is found. Remember a tree might appear as a circle and a line—but not *any* circle or *any* line. The size of the circle, the position, length, and width of the line must express an "idea" of a tree. A square might represent a house, a boat, or a leaf, but only because of its relationship to other basic shapes in the composition. When you reduce a natural object to its simplest geometric state, you must be sensitive to the slightest variation in spacing. To create extreme simplicity requires the most concentrated effort. Now try for an elaborate but fascinating complicity of geometric lines, angles, and shapes. Let this have a subject such as "Tall forests, tenements, sailboats, or light rays." Fig. 141. Superfluous elements must be avoided and only those lines used which enhance the idea. Crossings of lines and areas, transparencies and counterchange (alternating colors as they overlap), are a part of your thinking when designing geometrically. Add color changes, space, receding values, emphasis, and movement, and even though we have restricted our design to mechanical curves and straight lines our design can be remarkably "vital."

Fig. 141. Richard D. Kozlow, "Palmero," A geometric interpretation of objects such as buildings must still embody the vital elements of distribution, spacing, and selection.

The ruler and compass should be used for this work. Mechanical lines are not intended to be drawn freehand.

Something should be said about color in these various styles. In the case of the stylized conceptions, the color may be sophisticated and less obvious than in the naturalistic. The conventional design may be less dramatic in color—less forceful. The geometric style, however, suggests strong bold contrasts. Our basic geometric shapes seem to call for vigorous basic colors, perhaps sharply contrasted with black and white. This must not be taken as a set of rules, for immediately we can think of examples quite to the contrary. Simply because geometric African bark cloth designs *are* strong colors with black and white, the use of soft hues as seen in some contemporary geometric paintings is not discredited.

Fig. 142. Margaret De Patta, "Pendant." An outstanding example of geometric design is shown in this handsome piece of contemporary jewelry. Rutilated quartz and silver add the flash of highlights.

We have concerned ourselves with flat areas of color, and the importance of two-dimensional geometric study cannot be overstressed. Mosaics and some enamels can benefit by this study. Jewelry and other enameled shapes, which utilize the geometric style three-dimensionally, follow similar rules, Fig. 142. In flat designs, for example, we can add strength and emphasis to our geometric pattern by the simple expedient of shading some areas. Think of some planes as being overlapped by others, and possibly shade those in back with darker values of the same color. The planes should exist forward and backward in the design even though they are still two-dimensional in character. Shading around certain areas as halations gives another effect, and shading may also tend to tip the planes as though they were turned away from the source of light.

ABSTRACT STYLE

Our final step in designing from a natural object relies upon abstract interpretation. In this instance we go as far from representation as it is possible to go. Nothing remains of the original subject but a symbol or an implication of its major characteristics. As we have progressed with these five ways of interpreting the subject more is required of the artist's imagination—more of the personal feeling about that subject is brought into the design. It is certainly not true that one type of design is "*easier*" to do than another.

Although no treatise can presume to give the artist rules for making an abstract design from literal subject matter, it might be of help to list the kinds of freedom he has.

First, the actual shape or contour is no longer of primary importance. Many phenomena such as smoke, clouds, water, or fire have no positive shape. The eye recognizes them only as constantly moving symbols, and these symbols are nothing more than preconceived interpretations by artists. Therefore, we have a right to represent these amorphous, shapeless masses *idealistically.* Abstraction of these subjects is readily accepted by the layman, but when the same idealistic interpretation is applied to more concrete subjects such as animals, figures, buildings, and so on, the artist is often questioned or misunderstood. In designing, one should be allowed to interpret *any* subject in an abstract way.

Secondly, anatomy or structure is purposely misplaced or distorted and sometimes destroyed for the sake of a stronger symbolic statement. This is another way in which the contemporary designer who works abstractly is liberated from conventionality. We might take a leaf as a subject. In a stylized leaf we elongated and exaggerated the shapes but retained the original structure. In the formal or conventional leaf there was still a use of struc-

Fig. 143. "Le Cyprès Noir," Aubusson tapestry after a design by M. Prassinos. In this contemporary French tapestry monotony has been skillfully avoided by varying the shape of each "spot."

ture (how it is built) but it was repeated exactly on the left and right side of a center line. The geometric leaf showed less concern for the structure; there was more invention with the elements such as mass, midrib, and auxiliary ribs. Now, in the abstract leaf none of the foregoing structural elements need to be placed in proper relation to the leaf as we know it. The leaf becomes indefinite, and structure is arbitrarily placed according to the designer's will.

It is evident that to consciously misplace anatomical structure, the designer-craftsman should first have a working knowledge of that structure. Paintings by important abstractionists demonstrate this fact, Fig. 144. Their research about a subject gives their abstract interpretation of it greater conviction and meaning.

In order to show the extreme simplification needed in our abstract design we must have some feeling about it—one way or another. It is not possible to reduce a zebra to an abstract group-

Fig. 144. Morris Graves, "Wounded Scoter." A purely abstract interpretation of a bird-form. The artist, entirely aware of the bird's actual *structure, does not choose to make use of it per se.*

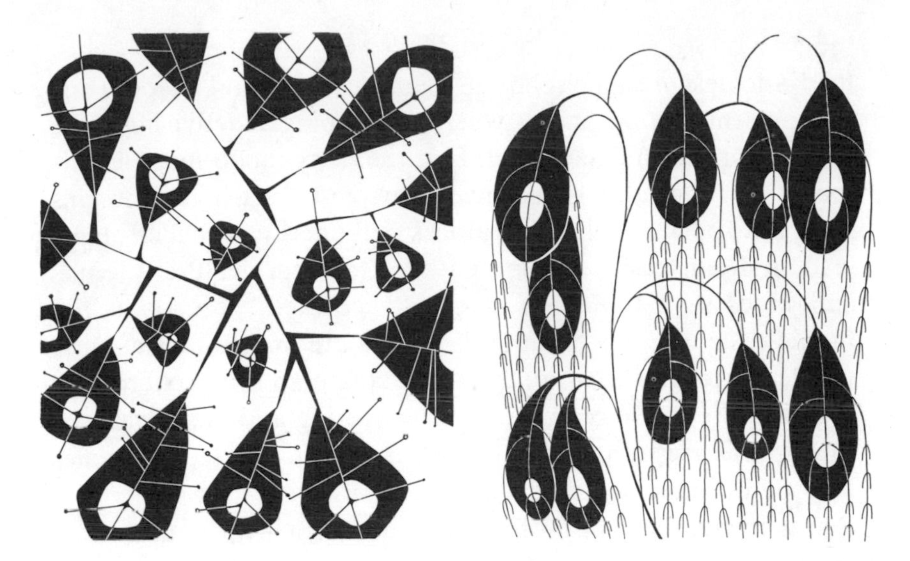

Fig. 145. On the left, the leaf shapes seem to "explode" from the stem, other branches and stems "shoot" in every direction with a kind of "impatient" energy. Fig. 146. The curves bend downward, the leaf shapes hang listlessly, and there is a lack of life.

ing of stripes (Fig. 147), unless the artist feels that way about the subject. He feels that, to him, these are the most dynamic, predominant, and expressive characteristics. These affect him most. If, by a few lines, suggestive masses of color, or textures, he can portray his impression without further detail, he is that much more ingenious.

Movement, whether expressed or implied, means the difference between dynamic and static design. Movement is not always created by the use of swirling curved lines. Sometimes the activated surface treatment gives a sense of movement or aliveness as in the case of Byzantine mosaics. Much depends on the way the tesserae are placed and the freedom of shapes and colors. The surface seems to move.

Mood, or emotional content, in any of these crafts is achieved not only through color and values. We know that light, facile, pastoral, feminine colors produce a different mood than heavy, dark, murky, dingy colors. But mood can also be the result of the basic design shapes chosen. Vigorous lines and shapes (Fig. 145) present a living quality, whereas drooping, inactive lines give a wilted or sentimental mood, Fig. 146. Any mood may be portrayed so long as it is the invention of the artist. All designs need not sparkle with cheerfulness and energy, as cheerfulness in design can easily become coy and saccharine. Pretty pinks and blues seen too often in our "decorated" tea rooms are in bad taste not only because the colors are insipid, but because the decorator has tried too hard to "create an atmosphere." By contrast, the subtle coloring of wall covering and materials used in display cases of our best contemporary art museums creates a mood of refinement and sophistication.

It is hoped that our abstract design, whether for a mosaic, an enameled tray, or piece of jewelry, will express some individual mood by the manner in which we have combined colors, values, shapes, and lines.

Fig. 147. The stripes of the zebra become a symbol which supersedes anatomical acceptance for the abstract designer. The "stripeyness" stands for the zebra.

CHAPTER VII

DESIGN IN PANELS, MURALS, AND BOXES

The nonobjective approach, composition

THE design for a covered box, a panel, either framed or mounted, and a mural decoration involves principles which have not yet been discussed in detail. These are the principles of composing within a given area, and for a particular function.

There are special problems as well as great possibilities in designing a panel for the cover or lid of a box, whether it be wood, metal, or ceramic. Naturally, function must come first—where will it be seen?—how will it be used? If it is a cigarette box it could be cylindrical, oblong, and flat, or higher and more like a cube. But the designer must not become "emotionally" involved with some whimsy of color and pattern and forget to measure the cigarette, or consider how many cigarettes the box will hold. He should consider what kind of decor and in what kind of room the box is intended.

First let us decide whether the box-cover design will be formal or informal (structural or nonstructural). Second, is the lid to be hinged or not hinged? If the cover is hinged, the design must "read" when viewed from the edge opposite the hinge, Fig. 148. If it is an unhinged cover, the design should not be "one-way-up,"

Fig. 148. Joseph Trippetti, "The Bachelor's Dinner." This enamel could be adapted as a "one-way-up" panel on a box hinged at the top.

but be equally effective from any view. This is very important even though the design is purely nonobjective. In other words the design should not appear "upside down" when held in one position, Fig. 149. No one cares to take time to think how a cover is to be replaced on a box.

With a round cover for a cylindrical box it might be in better taste to decide on a very simple or conventional design. A plain color could be used effectively, especially if there is a striking but contrasting color used for the interior of the box. This gives a second pleasure to the user as he opens the box.

Height, length, and width or diameter in an interesting relation to each other are all part of the designer's problem. If possible, try to avoid a monotonous duplication of dimensions, such as the height of the box being the same as the width or length. Exact multiples of dimensions, such as length being twice the width, etc., are almost sure to be less interesting than more subtle relationships. *Make a model,* even if you do it roughly; suggest the colors for your cover and the color of the material for the box. Most artists and craftsmen do not visualize from plan drawings nearly as well as architects or carpenters.

In regard to designing a panel or mural, here again the consideration for the use of the panel, whether it will be placed in a hospital, cocktail bar, or church—whether it should be quiet, spirited, or dignified—is as much a part of the designer's problem as arranging shapes and colors in their proper juxtaposition.

Consider the effectiveness of the proportions of the rectangle. Again, try not to arrive at a panel which is two, three, or four squares long. The proportions have much to do with whether the rectangle is "interesting" or "tiresome." Try a panel which is two

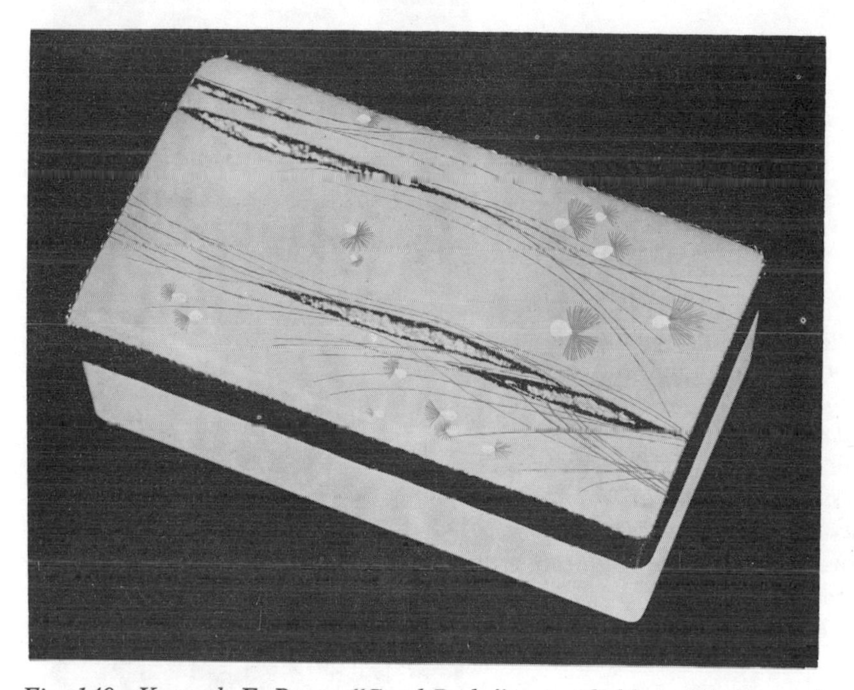

Fig. 149. Kenneth F. Bates, "Seed Pods," enameled box. This type of design is more appropriate for a box which is not hinged.

and four-fifths squares long, three and one-third squares long or something similar. Fig. 58.

Even though the subject of "Dynamic Symmetry" is seldom taught today, especially as a rule for design (books on Dynamic Symmetry can be found in any library), it has left us with one rule which it is good to remember. This concerns the place within the rectangle where an accent may fall. This place is known as the "golden cut." If you are thinking of a rectangle horizontally the golden cut will fall at a place more than two-thirds and less than three-quarters along its length. In analyzing hundreds of pictures or panels, it is surprising to find how often the artist instinctively uses this place for an accent, Fig. 150.

Fig. 150. Peter Paul Dubaniewicz, "Seashore Gear." This is an example of how the professional artist may instinctively place a strategic accent directly on the "golden cut" (see text). The center of the life saver falls exactly on a point greater than two-thirds and less than three-quarters of the length of the panel.

Figs. 151, 152, 153. Ways of filling space. From top to bottom "opposing forces"; a serpentine line which tends to fill the entire area; a pyramidal mass.

Fig. 154. Realistic rendering of a fox.

Fig. 155. Stylization of a fox.

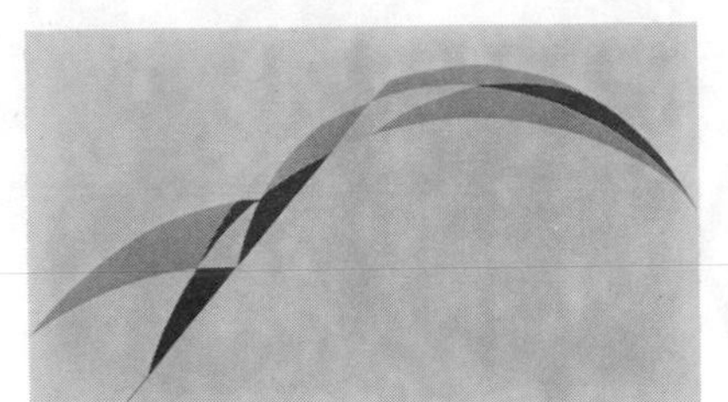

Fig. 156. Geometric interpretation of a fox.

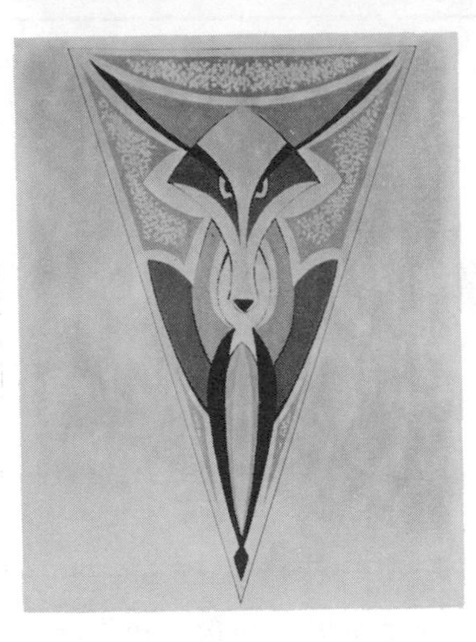

Fig. 157. Conventionalized rendering of a fox.

Fig. 158. Abstraction of a fox.

The rhythm within the panel can take many forms. Here are a few suggestions: (1) processional; (2) opposing forces, Fig. 151; (3) serpentine path from one end to the other, Fig. 152; (4) series of spots; (5) allover texture, Fig. 54; (6) pyramidal or lunar, Fig. 153. In each case the intention is to lead the eye along the rectangle instead of stopping the rhythmical movement or isolating one part of the panel from the remainder.

Fig. 159. The pattern you observe formed by maple leaves against the sky may be the starting point of a design.

NONOBJECTIVE STYLE

In this chapter we come to another style, *nonobjective.* It follows our sequence of studies from realism to abstraction, but actually, it carries design beyond the realm of subject matter entirely. The preceding five styles (realistic, Fig. 154; stylized, Fig. 155, conventional, Fig. 157; geometric, Fig. 156; and abstract, Fig. 158) demand more and more imagination and inventiveness on the part of the artist. Nonobjective art is based purely on imagination with no particular subject to be interpreted. This is solely a design for design's sake needing no further justification other than that. (Fig. 59.)

To commence the nonobjective design, establish some group of lines or combination of shapes and colors as the foundation for your composition. Try to find this grouping accidentally through some experience in everyday life. Perhaps a kaleidoscopic intermingling of colors in the costumes of a crowd of people; the strange shapes made by oil on puddles of water; or patterns formed by leaves as you look up from under a maple tree, Fig. 159. Any such experience may be the starting point for one's imagination. This constitutes the original scribble. Now change it, vary it, play with it until some satisfaction in its possible development (its design potential is found). Whether we have the completed design in our "mind's eye" before we start, or whether we let it develop is immaterial. It is most important, however, that a craftsman have a clear idea of his design and how it relates to the task at hand (perhaps more so than the painter). He must decide on the material, such as wood, enamel, or silver, as well as the design motif.

Start making the nonobjective design—get out brushes, paper, sticks, and palette knives. Open all the colors, not simply one or two, in the set of tempera paints, just as an oil painter has all of the colors in readiness around the palette.

Instead of dipping into the temperas as they are presented to us in their primary and secondary hues, first make admixtures of various sorts which will be more inspiring than the "straight" colors. In their original state these temperas are only "pigments" *for making* colors. Some knowledge of color theory is needed at this point (reread Munsell Color Theory, Chapter IV), otherwise

Fig. 160. "Growing" from the frame of the picture is a trait to be avoided, if possible. Fig. 161. The same elements—not "growing" from the edge—give more inner strength, greater unity.

our color schemes will appear crude and amateurish. Primitive designs and children's paintings have great charm because of their use of primary color, but this represents only one phase of color. Intelligent exploration with color is more to be desired now.

After admixtures are found, then experiment by putting combinations, juxtapositions, and varying proportions of these together. Our basic study of spots, lines, and masses will be an aid to our thinking though this should not be followed too academically. The nonobjective design must not look "contrived," it must look "free." The design must have looseness, freedom, and expressiveness if it is to be contemporary, and appeal to others.

Who is to say when the nonobjective design is finished or has

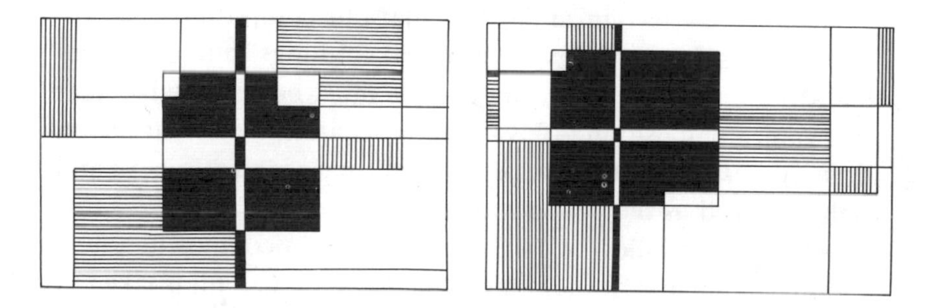

Fig. 162. With major elements in the center, the composition lacks interest. Fig. 163. The same elements placed off center give greater freedom and interest to the composition.

enough "in it" or enough left out? Neither instructor nor textbook can answer this question. The decision rests entirely with the artist.

The word "composition" is a confusing term. To be sure, we are composing the moment we select one line or one shape to go with another. But, up to this time we have concentrated upon the construction of motifs, and their application to various uses. Not too much concern has been placed upon how they exist within a given boundary or specific panel.

The composition of a stated area poses individual problems. Each area (square, circle, vertical or horizontal rectangle) must be designed to exist for what it is. If the circle suggests movement in flowing lines which relate to the curved contour, then straight, angular configurations may work better in a square. A vertical rectangle can stress the verticality of the area, and a horizontal rectangle contain horizontal movement, especially if this is the intent of the artist. However, these are not rules to be followed blindly. One suggestion for designing within a circle is to concentrate upon the area of the circle until one "feels" the boundary of it, and its related movements within. By bending a shape or line near the circumference, sometimes one can lead the eye around, rather than out of, the circle. Also a line can appear to go out of the circle in one place and re-enter it somewhere else.

We will soon recognize the fact that our composition is composed of positive and negative areas (the "things" and the spaces left around the "things"). These areas must be arranged so that the whole composition holds together as a unit. Concentrate on these spaces or negative shapes so that they are as attractive and well arranged as the positive areas.

Setting down rules for "what not to do" in composition may seem pedantic, but at the same time it can be helpful if taken in the right spirit. Here are a few: (1) Try not to grow things from the edge, or to use the edge of the composition as the horizon line, or ground line, Figs. 160, 161. (2) Greater freedom is ex-

Fig. 164. Shapes whose edges are parallel to the sides of a composition present a static quality. Fig. 165. The same shapes have more action and movement, when their edges are not parallel to the frame.

pressed by *not* placing a strong interest at the center or on the central axis, either vertically or horizontally, Figs. 162, 163. (3) Elements whose axes or contours are parallel to the sides of the composition are more static than those which are not so related to the frame, Figs. 164, 165. (4) By pointing shapes directly out of the corner, the eye may be led away from the main interest, Figs. 166, 167. (5) Try not to create shapes which are tangent to themselves or to the edges of the composition unless you intend to create a feeling of tension, Figs. 168, 169. (6) If an object is nearer the edge of the composition than it is to other

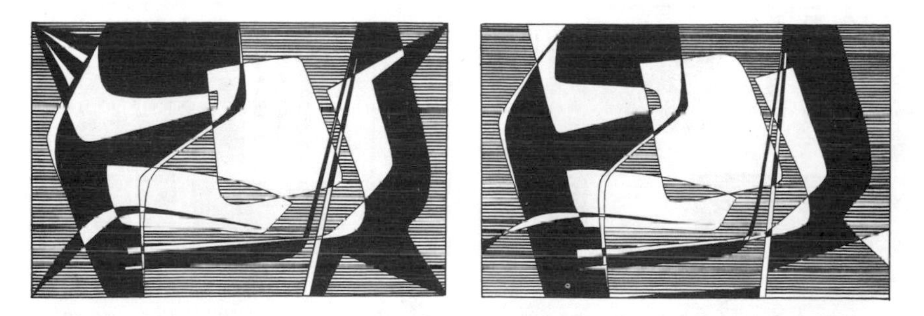

Fig. 166. Shapes which point directly out the corners of the composition lead the eye away from the main interest. The picture tends to fall apart. Fig. 167. The eye is brought back into the picture by not allowing shapes to point directly out the corners.

Fig. 168. Shapes which are tangent in a composition are apt to create too much tension. Fig. 169. When the same shapes are not tangent a more restful feeling is attained.

objects within the picture, the design often lacks unity. Generally speaking, the sum total of space between objects should be less than the sum total of space which surrounds them as a group, Figs. 170, 171.

If a design student searches for all the rules needed to assure his success with composition he will never find them, for each situation is unique and has to be solved individually. There will always be an artist of integrity who will be able to break the rules successfully. Remember that the unexpected (breaking the rule) is more interesting than the expected, and the impossible more exciting than the possible. Only your own "feeling" will tell you when a composition holds together and when it falls apart.

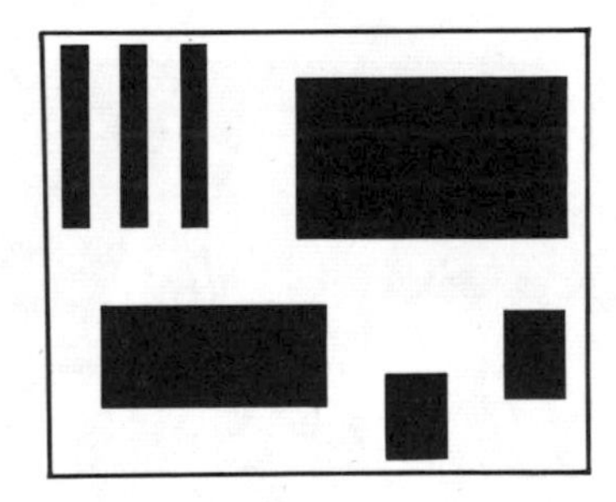

Fig. 170. The composition on the left lacks unity because: (1) The objects are nearer the edge than they are to each other. (2) The sum total of square inches between the objects is greater than the total of square inches around the objects as a group. Fig. 171. This composition holds together better as a unit.

CHAPTER VIII

DESIGN DEVELOPMENT

Function, research, inspiration, and fluency

IN THIS book we have covered only the brief groundwork for design thinking. We have concentrated upon two-dimensional or flat design, its origin, development, and application to three-dimensional objects. There is a world ahead in the study of objects as they exist in space, and in the function of new materials which are invented every day. We must get used to automobiles which float above the ground, and cantilever surfaces which seem to be unsupported. We might reword the subtitle of this chapter as: "What is the design for (function), how have other civilizations solved similar problems (research), where can we get new ideas (inspiration), and what is the value of making more than one trial (fluency)?"

Consider, for example, the judgment that your design will receive. The prime factor in the mind of the juror, critic, and layman will undoubtedly be the appropriateness of the design to the situation for which it was created, or *function.* Function is concerned with how successfully an abstract area of color is placed in a certain part of a picture as much as it is with how large a handle is to a coffee cup. This, then, is the first criterion for judgment. The second concerns what kind of a shape, color, or combination of these was chosen by the artist in the first place. This, we will call "taste." Because it seems quite probable that these judgments will also be based somewhat on academic principles of basic design, it is evident that the artist should recognize their value. How often has an art student refused to rely on design principles for fear that he would be called "academic" and then submitted his work for professional criticism only to hear these remarks: "This shape is too large, that shape lacks good proportions, it lacks rhythm, it is out of balance"?

Who can say what is a good shape or an ugly shape? It comes back to function. "It is a good shape for that purpose," or "it is ugly in that relationship." If a table is so designed that it functions as a table, it stands a better chance of being a good design than one which does not, although function alone is not all that is required. A table, automobile, or tea cup is often originally conceived in the mind of the designer as an arrangement of

Fig. 172. Wallace Harrison, architect. First Presbyterian Church, Stamford, Conn. A fascinating example of contemporary architecture. No planes are at right angles or parallel to the ground.

lines, spots, and masses. The fact that the nonobjective artist exposes these elements (or rather, stops the painting when they are satisfactorily arranged) is no reason for the layman to think that the table or the tea cup were not started in the same manner. They must both be functional in the last analysis.

An architect may feel the monotony of creating buildings where every part of the structure is at right angles to another part. Consequently, we have examples of architectural experiments, some good, some questionable, where the roof lines are not parallel to the ground and the uprights are not at right angles to the plane of the ground, Fig. 172. Such experiments will be judged by the same criteria as the picture or coffee table. Does it function, and is it in good taste in the opinion of those who are sensitive to the laws of stability, proportion, balance, etc.? It is hoped, of course, that those who feel these laws are also flexible enough to appreciate the greater architect who can shrewdly but successfully break the academic rules.

"Exercises" in art are quite deadly and entirely different from the laboratory experimentation which we will call "research." Rather than thinking that "art can be fun" (a point of view which unfortunately has sold too many books to the amateur), think of art as a tremendously complex and challenging activity that will warrant most serious concentration. Research in basic design should not be grim, neither should it be used as a therapeutic cure for hypertension. *One must be serious, but not too serious, disciplined but not overdisciplined!* Our interest in research must carry us into the physical world with a wonderment about nature, and also into the great periods of history. To designers, some periods are more valuable than others. The following partial list includes some of the most exciting design inspirations of all time! Egyptian sculpture, Fig. 122; Greek stylization (especially horses), Fig. 175; Northwest Indian totem pole motifs, Fig. 173; Persian illuminated manuscripts, Fig. 97; Byzantine jewelry and enamels, and primitive African sculpture, Fig. 174. It is hard to say what not to look at in the

Fig. 173. A Northwest Indian totem pole design.

Fig. 174. African "Mule's Head," French Sudan.

Fig. 175. Athenian Amphora 525 B.C. Stylization at its best is found in Greek vase painting.

Fig. 176. Chester Beach, "Unveiling of Dawn." Both the title and the smooth marble treatment appear too sentimental for most contemporary artists. Fig. 177. "Studio Stairway." The Art Nouveau period produced designs which seem strange to us today.

way of research. The influence of the Paris Exposition of 1900, for example, may have set in motion what seems to us some of the most fantastic and flamboyant designs imaginable, Fig. 177. Stephan Madsen's *Sources of Art Nouveau,* George Wittenborn, Inc., 1955, New York, describes this period from 1898 to 1905 when nation after nation indulged in the swirling-line form of decoration. In recent times there has been a re-evaluation of this period in our history, and it would strengthen us as design students to study the Art Nouveau style as well as the sculpture in the United States from about 1900 to 1910, Fig. 176. Nevertheless, such an abundance of smooth, sterile forms in the sculpture and stiff formulated outlines in the decoration of this period seems far removed from our fresh, individualistic attitude about design today.

The ostentatious display of skills without regard to sensitivity and taste is not the aim of the artist. An artist does not merely search nature for examples of design which when interpreted by

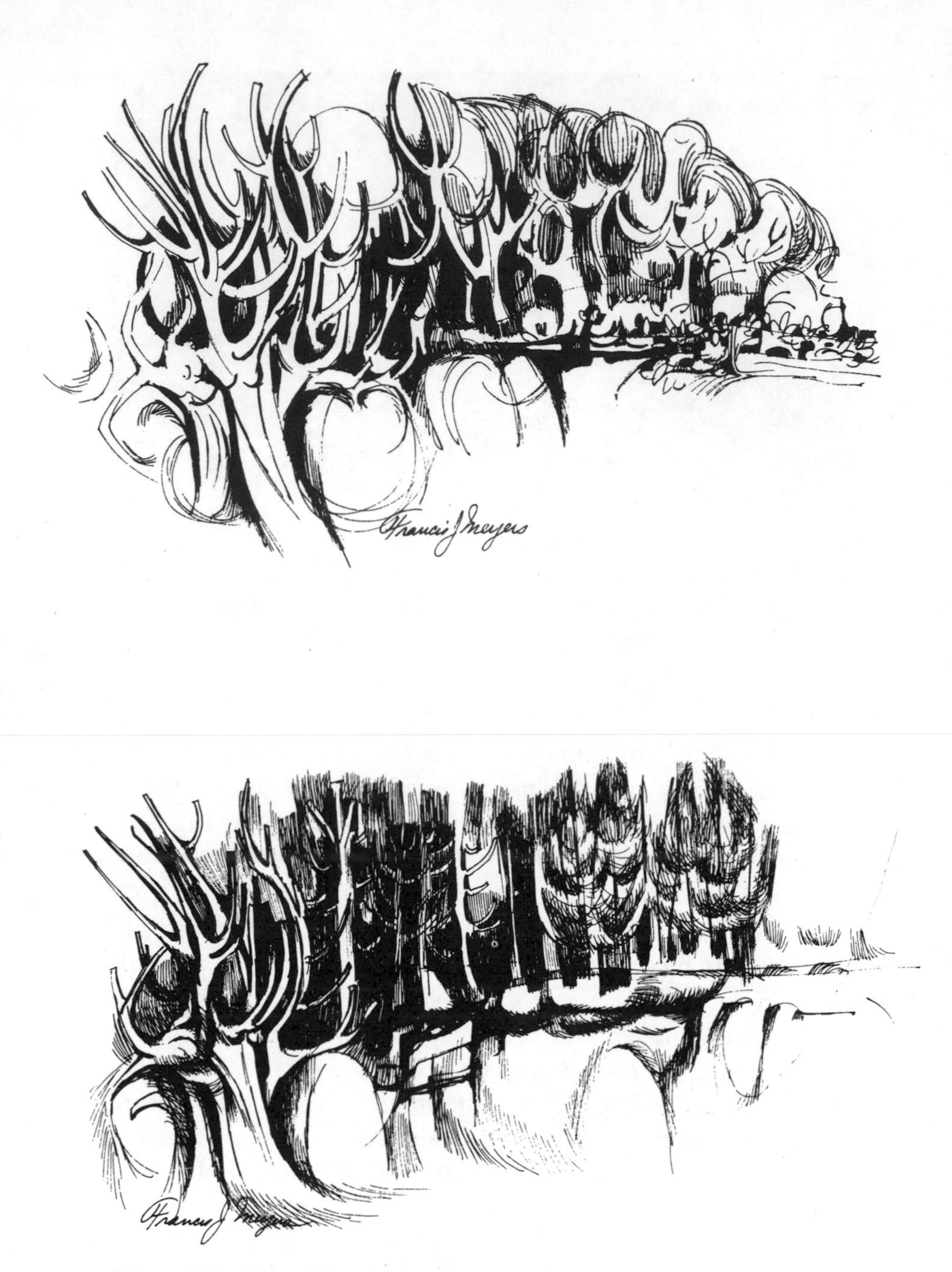

Figs. 178, 179, 180, 181. Francis Meyers, "Studies of Trees." This superb group of drawings no longer constitutes an "exercise," but rep-

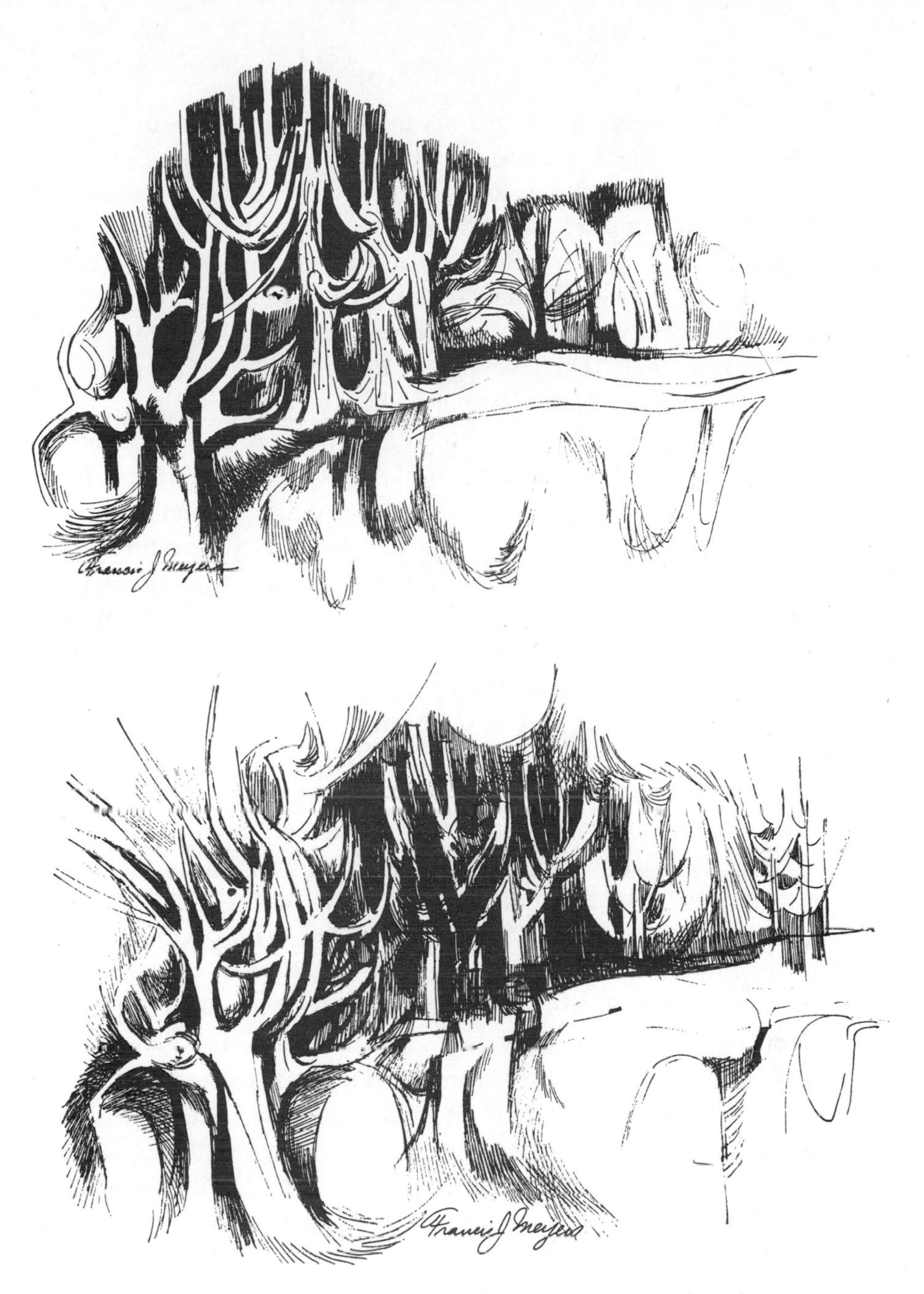

resents an exploration that clearly demonstrates "fluency" in design. Close examination shows that no detail of the trees is actually identical.

him will engender praise for his talents. Research is quite another thing. The artist constantly collects ideas, impressions, and reactions from everything around him. These, in turn, are stored away in his mind, to be used or not, as the inspiration arises. Research, in a more specific way, implies making pencil notes in a notebook as well as mental notes. Art students are graded more stringently on their notebooks than on their classroom accomplishments. The layman and hobbyist should also keep a notebook of inspirations if he intends to fully enjoy his art. Our research can encompass anything or everything. It may possibly lead us to something as commonplace as a cobweb. Take a few moments to study the cobweb. It is an exquisite design from the point of view of sensitivity, variation, simplicity, and function. It does not have to be explained. It is there for us to enjoy, not only with our eyes but with our intellect as well. Look for those subtle imperfections in the design of a cobweb which make the difference between mathematical precision and art.

As you train your eyes to see better, your designs are bound to increase in conviction and content. Closely allied with being inspired by the design potential of all life about us is our own fascination in experimentation. First we record some significant incident or object which has been an inspiration to us, but here the more vital process of creative designing begins. We will speak of this as "design fluency." By that is meant the unending search for variation upon a given theme. An artist is ever cognizant of this infinite variation in all existence, and therefore feels impelled to exercise variation in his own work. He finds that by making innumerable experiments he has enlarged his opportunity to exercise his discrimination. He never stops with the first trial! His constant search is like a continuous journey through life, the ending of which would be less pleasant than its continuation. He discovers the fact, for instance, that the same basic tree form can be changed in hundreds of ways and still embody his individualistic style. Figs. 178, 179, 180, and 181.

Fig. 183. Charles Burchfield, "Church Bells Ringing, Rainy Winter Night," water color. The work of this internationally known artist is done in "a manner which is his, and his alone."

Fluency, of course, implies "ease of doing" or skill, about which we have said little in this book, and yet it goes without saying that this is an accomplishment for which every mature artist strives. The beginner, also, must realize that making one design is inevitably the result of choosing from many variations of that design.

First and last, then, the study of basic design is deeply concerned with the infinite variation of natural phenomena. To live in wonderment, and to recognize this phenomena as his birthright is the artist's role. He should consider it both a privilege and a duty to interpret life in a manner which is his, and his alone.

✤ BIBLIOGRAPHY

Adam, Leonhard, *Nordwestamerikanische Indianerkunst,* Orbis Pictus/ Weltkunst-Bücherei, Band 17, Ernst Wasmuth A. G., Berlin, 1923.

Albers, Josef, *American Abstract Artists,* The Ram Press, New York, 1946.

Archer, W. G., ed., *Indian Painting,* Oxford University Press, New York, 1957.

Bates, Kenneth F., *Enameling: Principles and Practice,* The World Publishing Co., Cleveland and New York, 1951.

Bernier, George and Rosamont, eds., *The Selective Eye,* Reynal and Co., New York, 1956–57.

Biederman, Charles, *Art as the Evolution of Visual Knowledge,* Charles Biederman, Red Wing, Minn., 1948.

Blumenau, Lili, *Art and Craft of Hand Weaving,* Crown Publishing Co., New York, 1955.

Bowra, C. M., *The Greek Experience,* The World Publishing Co., Cleveland and New York, 1957.

Burris-Meyers, Elizabeth, *Historic Guide to Color,* W. Helburn Inc., New York, 1947.

Cane, Florence, *The Artist in Each of Us,* Pantheon Books, Inc., New York, 1951.

Chase, Lynwood M., *Look at Life,* Alfred A. Knopf, New York, 1940.

Dobkin, Alexander, *Principles of Figure Drawing,* The World Publishing Co., Cleveland and New York, 1952.

Doering, Heinrich U., *The Art of Ancient Peru,* Frederick A. Praeger, New York, 1952.

Emerson, Sybil, *Design, A Creative Approach,* International Textbook Co., Scranton, 1953.

Faulkner, Ray, *Art Today,* 3rd ed., Henry Holt and Co., New York, 1956.

Gardner, Helen, *Art Through the Ages,* 4th ed., Harcourt, Brace and Co., New York, 1959.

Gump, Richard, *Good Taste Costs No More,* Doubleday and Co., New York, 1951.

Hepworth, Barbara, *Carvings and Drawings,* Lund Humphries & Co. Ltd., London, 1952.

Janus, Horst, *Nature as Architect,* Frederick Ungar Publishing Co., New York, 1957.

Jenkins, Louisa, and Mills, Barbara, *Art of Making Mosaics,* D. Van Nostrand Co., Inc., New York, 1957.

The Journal of Aesthetics and Art Criticism, Vol. XVI, No. 1, Sept., 1957.

Kepes, Gyorgy, *Language of Vision,* Paul Theobald, Chicago, 1944.

———, *The New Landscape,* Paul Theobald, Chicago, 1956.

Laport, Louis-Jacques, *Panorama du Micro-Monde,* Librairie Grund, Paris, 1949.

Lenning, Henry F., *The Art Nouveau,* Martinus Nijhoff, The Hague, 1951.

Madsen, Stephan Tschudi, *Sources of Art Nouveau,* George Wittenborn, Inc., New York, 1955.

Malraux, André, *Museum Without Walls,* Pantheon Books, Inc., New York, 1949.

———, *The Twilight of the Absolute,* Pantheon Books, Inc., New York, 1950.

Martin, Charles, *How To Make Modern Jewelry,* Museum of Modern Art, New York, 1949.

Maryon, Herbert, *Metalwork and Enameling,* Dover Publications, New York, 1955.

Moholy-Nagy, Laszlo, *The New Vision,* Wittenborn & Co., New York, 1946.

———, *Vision and Motion,* Paul Theobald, Chicago, 1946.

Munro, Thomas, "Aesthetics and the Artist," *The Journal of Aesthetics and Art Criticism,* Vol. XI, No. 8, June, 1953.

———, *The Arts and Their Interrelations,* The Liberal Arts Press, New York, 1949.

Nelson, George, *Problems in Design,* Whitney Publications, Inc., New York, 1957.

Newton, Norman T., *An Approach to Design,* Addison Wesley Press, Cambridge, Mass., 1951.

Pack, Greta, *Jewelry and Enameling,* D. Van Nostrand Co., Inc., New York, 1941.

Pope, Arthur Upham, *Masterpieces of Persian Art,* The Dryden Press, New York, 1945.

Reinach, S., *Apollo,* Charles Scribner's Sons, New York, 1922.

Reumuth, Horst, *Unter der Mikrowelt,* Konrodin-Verlag, Robert Kohlhammer, Stuttgart, 1954.

Rogers, Frances and Beard, Alice, *5000 Years of Gems and Jewelry,* Frederick A. Stokes Co., New York, 1940.

Saarinen, Eliel, *Search for Form,* Reinhold Publishing Co., New York, 1948.

Scott, Robert Gillam, *Design Fundamentals,* McGraw-Hill Book Co., New York, 1951.

Shahn, Ben, *The Shape of Content,* Harvard University Press, Cambridge, Mass., 1957.

Shippan-Sha, Bijutsu, *Noguchi,* Tokyo, 1953.

Slobodkin, Louis, *Sculpture: Principles and Practice,* The World Publishing Co., Cleveland and New York, 1949.

Slomann, Vilhelm, *Bizarre Designs in Silks,* Ejnar Munksgaard, Copenhagen, 1953.

Teague, Walter Dorwin, *Design This Day,* Harcourt, Brace & Co., New York, 1940.

Texture and Pattern, Teaching Portfolio, No. 2, Museum of Modern Art, New York, 1949.

Tucker, Allen, *Design and the Idea,* Oxford University Press, New York, 1939.

Watkins, C. Law, *The Language of Design,* Phillips Memorial Gallery, Washington, D. C., 1946.

Watson, Baker W., *World Beneath the Microscope,* The Studios Publications, Inc., New York, 1935.

Winter, Edward, *Enamel Art on Metals,* Watson-Guptill Publications, Inc., New York, 1958.

Zervos, Christian, *Constantin Brancusi,* Cahiers d'Art, Paris, 1957.

Zvenigorodskoi, A. V., *Histoire et Monuments des Emaux Byzantins,* N. Kondakow, Frankfort on Main (Pierpont Morgan Collection), 1892.

ACKNOWLEDGMENTS

The author is grateful for permission to reproduce the works represented in this book through the courtesy of the people and institutions named. (Students' works are indicated by an asterisk.)

American Craftsmen's Council, 60, 69, 127, 143
  (Photo: William Ryan), 64
  (Photo: Walter Rosenblum), 71
  (Photo: Charles Uhl), 142
A. Appleby,* 115
D. Attie,* 26, 52, 59
Brooklyn Museum, 47
Butler Institute of American Art, 108, 110, 141
C. Chisman,* 50
The Cleveland Museum of Art
  Dudley P. Allen Collection, 68
  J. H. Wade Collection, 82, 97
  Mr. and Mrs. Ralph King Collection, 109
  Gift of Hanna Fund, 111
  Hinman B. Hurlbut Collection, 114
  Silver Jubilee Treasure Fund, Contributions of the Public to the Wishing Well, 131
  Gift of Mrs. R. Henry Norweb, Mrs. A. S. Ingalls, with additions from the John L. Severance Fund, 132
  Gift of Gamblers in Modern Art, 144
  James Albert Ford Memorial, 174
  In Memory of Henry B. Keller, 183
Cleveland Museum of Natural History, 139
S. Cornell,* 21
Craft Horizons, 83
  (Photo: Ernest Lowe), 56
Cranbrook Foundation (Photo: Harvey Croze), 121
J. Cullinan,* 20
R. Deardoff,* 17
S. Denek,* 100
T. Dunn,* 55
Felix Landau Gallery, 106
E. Freska,* 19, 49
M. Gelin,* 44
K. Gergo,* 147
J. Hawthorne,* 11, 12, 13, 14
Hexter Fabrics, 70
G. Ilg,* 154, 155, 156, 157, 158
R. Kay,* 84
N. Larson,* 63
Stephan Tschudi Madsen, Oslo, Norway, 177
R. Mahoney,* 62
Martin Studios (Photo), 148
The Metropolitan Museum of Art
  Rogers Fund, 1934, 122
  Rogers Fund, 1906, 175
  Gift of Mr. and Mrs. George W. Davison, 1943, 176
J. Miller,* 24, 51
Mary Mosgo, 125
The Museum of Modern Art, 136
Collection, The Museum of Modern Art, New York, 15, 37, 107, 140
  Gift of Edgar Kaufmann, 53
  Gift of Mrs. John D. Rockefeller, Jr., 119
The Museum of Primitive Art, 1
R. Newman,* 30
K. Osterhus,* 18
Pan American Union, 38
C. Phillips,* 101
S. Pizziferato,* 102
P. Postma,* 43
Svetozar Radakovich (Photo: Charles Arnold and Terry Linquist), 130
E. Ruppe,* 112

R. Singerman,* 31
Wilhelm Sloman, *Bizarre Designs in Silk,* Copenhagen, 1953, 134
Syracuse Museum of Fine Arts, The National Ceramic Collection, 123
A. Tomcik,* 99
K. Torda,* 61
Utah State University Art Collection, 66
Waldorf, Mrs. E. J., Collection, Frontispiece
J. Wrobbel,* 54

INDEX

ABOUT THE AUTHOR

KENNETH F. BATES, was born in North Scituate, Massachusetts, in 1904. A graduate of the Massachusetts School of Art he continued his education in Europe, culminating with a period of study under Claude Lemunier at the Fontainebleau School of Fine Arts. Married and the father of three children, Mr. Bates now makes his home in Euclid, Ohio. He has guided and instructed art students in the theory of design for the past thirty-three years, and at present teaches design and enameling at the Cleveland Institute of Art. Among the many prizes he has received for his work have been a First Prize in Enamel at the Eleventh National Ceramic Exhibition in 1946, The Horace Potter Silver Medal for Excellence in Craftsmanship in both 1949 and 1957, and a Special Honor Award in 1957 from the Midwest Designer-Craftsmen. His work was exhibited at the New York World's Fair, 1939, the Golden Gate International Exposition, 1939, and the Brussels World's Fair in 1959, and in the latter year he was one of the major contributors to a retrospective exhibition of American Enameling held at the Museum of Contemporary Crafts in New York City. A frequent contributor to many journals in the field, Mr. Bates is the author of *Enameling: Principles and Practice* which was first published in 1951. In 1960, he was elected a Life Fellow of the International Institute of Arts and Letters.